D0041552

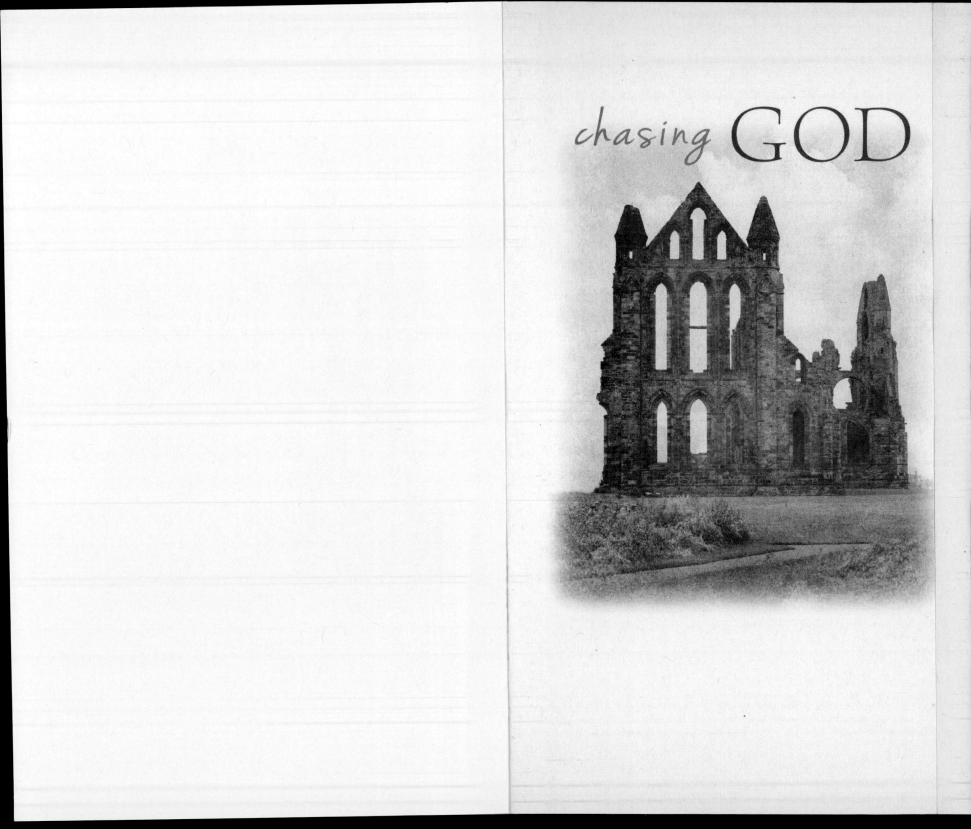

chasing GOD

chasing GOD

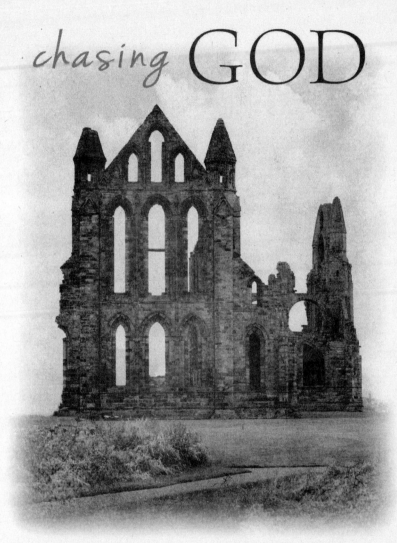

ANGIE SMITH

B&H
PUBLISHING GROUP
NASHVILLE, TENNESSEE

Copyright © 2014 by Angie Smith

All rights reserved.

Printed in the United States of America

978-1-4336-7661-1

Published by B&H Publishing Group

Nashville, Tennessee

Dewey Decimal Classification: 248.843

Subject Heading: WOMEN \ CHRISTIAN LIFE \ GOD

Unless otherwise designated, Scripture quotations are from the English Standard Version, copyright © 2001 by Crossway Bibles, a publishing ministry of Good News Publishers.

Also used: the Holman Christian Standard Bible® (HCSB). Copyright © 1999, 2000, 2002, 2003, 2009 by Holman Bible Publishers. Used by permission.

1 2 3 4 5 6 7 8 9 • 18 17 16 15 14

To the only One
who could make me stop running—
thank You for loving me before I knew
how to love You in return.

An "impersonal God"—well and good. A subjective God of beauty, truth and goodness, inside our own heads—better still. A formless life-force surging through us, a vast power which we can tap—best of all. But God Himself, alive, pulling at the other end of the cord, perhaps approaching at an infinite speed, the hunter, king, husband—that is quite another matter. There comes a moment when the children who have been playing at burglars hush suddenly: was that a real footstep in the hall? There comes a moment when people who have been dabbling in religion ("Man's search for God!") suddenly draw back.

Supposing we really found Him?

We never meant it to come to that!

Worse still, supposing He had found us?

~ C. S. Lewis, *Miracles*

Contents

View Park Library
3854 W. 54th St.
Los Angeles, CA 90043-
2297
Phone: (323) 293-5371

Title: Chasing God
Item ID: 0112416897737
Date charged: 3/9/2018,
10:45
Date due: 3/30/2018,23:59

Total checkouts for session:
1
Total checkouts:1

Renew your items online.
Log in to: www.
colapublib.org

Caedmon

Behold, heaven and the highest heaven cannot contain you;
how much less this house that I have built!

~ 1 Kings 8:27

One can hardly deny the appeal of a good chase.

It's beautiful in concept: we seek after that which eludes us, longing for something just out of reach. Anticipation builds as our hearts beat faster, wondering if we are about to turn the final corner and catch the object of our affection.

Our minds are wild with possibility and we're intoxicated by the sense of adventure. Before we know it, we've forgotten the objective because we're caught up in the thrill of wondering.

Either that, or we simply give up and forego the chase altogether because we're exhausted and discouraged.

It can only end in one of two ways: either we *catch up* or we *give up*.

And despite the outcome, it's safe to say that our running was based on the presumption that we want something more than it wants us.

For most of my Christian life, I have been chasing God.

I have piled up commentaries, memorized scholar's words, and watched how others walk with Him, all the while keeping journals of the bread crumbs I think He's leaving for me as I go.

I've stacked up the "required" pile with false obligations and bloated assumptions, and I've scorned the mystery with my desperate need for control.

I know I'm not alone.

We try to fill in the gray instead of living in the black and white. We shape theology to suit our taste, our times, our situations, and our desires. It's the mess we've made by desiring to understand Him more than we want to know Him, and we're growing more exhausted than inspired every day.

The goal of this book is not to present you with a formula for living out Christianity. It's to offer my thoughts on the difference between looking *for* Him and looking *at* Him.

And maybe you, like me, have been spending your time going after the wrong objectives (without realizing it) and it's left you weary of the whole process. What was meant to be a gift has become an obligation, a source of guilt, or a way to fight fear.

I assure you, I have been there. And it took quite a bit of time on my knees before I realized I was needlessly exhausted and unsure of my role as a follower of Christ. Don't misunderstand me; we are not called to be passive in our journey with Christ. In fact, being a disciple of Christ necessitates that we press forward until we can hardly believe we can do it anymore. The problem comes when we use our energy in ways He never asked us to because we're more concerned with our own feeble sketches of God than we are with *God Himself.*

We rely on our standards, our rules, our opinions, our agendas, and our measurements of holiness instead of His. And as the books pile one on top of another, so do the questions.

It's the difference between following and chasing.

The key that finally turned the door of my faith was understanding that we are called to one and not the other.

We stare at the rest of the pew, wondering why we aren't as far along as they are, secretly resenting those who unswervingly claim their faith while we enter another Bible study group, hoping something will stick.

If I just do this, I'll catch Him.

My misguided understanding of responsibility, control, and ability led me to despair of all the wrong failures and to celebrate successes that God Himself doesn't recognize as such.

It's what happens when you try to use religion to fill in the gaps of your faith.

Religion is what we build with our own hands when we can't stand to feel like observers. And when it crumbles, we blame God. We have determined the man-made ceiling to be our own instead of the heavens themselves, and we have allowed our insatiable hunger for understanding to strangle the mystery we're supposed to embrace.

On the cover of this book, you'll see an image that has become a visual representation to me of what I've learned in the past few years. It is what remains of a Benedictine monastery built in AD 657 called "Whitby Abbey." It sits on a cliff overlooking the North Sea to one side and the small New Yorkshire town Whitby on the other.

It was made famous for a number of reasons: most notably that it was home to Caedmon, the earliest English poet whose name is known. According to the well-known writer and scholar Saint Bede, Caedmon was an illiterate lay brother who tended to the animals on the property. Caedmon was not well-versed in religion and one night as a harp was being passed around in a time of worship, he left the monastery to sleep outdoors with the animals because he was ashamed that he knew none of the songs nor even how to sing.

It was there in the fields that he had a dream in which someone approached him and asked him to sing "the beginning of all created things." At first he refused, but then composed a short poem, seemingly without the human capacity to do so. This hymn is recorded as the oldest English poem in existence, and is spectacular in its simplicity and inspired recognition of God. While Caedmon went on to live a long and devoted life to Christ, penning many other spectacular works, he is most remembered for the words given to him in the middle of the night on a hillside in England:

> *Now [we] must honour the guardian of heaven,*
> *the might of the architect, and his purpose, the*
> *   work of the father of glory.*
> *As he, the eternal lord, established the beginning*
> *   of wonders;*
> *he first created for the children of men*
> *heaven as a roof, the holy creator.*
> *Then the guardian of mankind,*
> *the eternal lord, afterwards appointed the*
> *   middle earth*
> *the lands for men, the Lord almighty.*

He is the Architect, and our lives were given only to thank Him for His creation. When we spend our time gazing at the church ceiling instead of His sky, we fail to do so.

Centuries later, only a fraction of what men created remains, as will always be the case.

It stands exactly as it should now.

Walls around to remind us of what was laid on solid foundation. Guides to keep the boundaries where they should rightfully be. A legacy of stories of ages past, of saints that walked before us, and the general shape of what God intended as the church.

One day I want to go there to see it. I imagine I would let my fingers trace the stones and think of what it must have been like to worship within the walls. I would surely think it was magnificent in form, and would appreciate the skill and dedication that went into the labor.

But I would see it for what it is—the skeleton of something that still lives.

I would enjoy the building, yes. But then I would lay on what was once the floor of a great cathedral, and looking up I would see only the night sky where a roof once blocked its splendor, and I would thank Him for loving me enough to teach me that I have long studied the wrong view.

I understand why Caedmon ran that night, and I probably would have as well.

I know little of the music, it seems. I always feel like the one who doesn't quite get it; the one who missed the part where everything lined up and the questions stopped. Maybe you feel the same, and you've come here beside me in the still of night because you want to hear from the Creator instead of the created.

If that's the case, I hope you'll hear the sounds that came to me when the melodies ceased, and the voice that whispered hope when the darkness fell.

The tender words of a loving Father, piercing the emptiness with His presence:

> *Stop running like mad because you don't know the music; lay in the wild grass while the stars dance instead.*

Forget what they've told you about Me and stop thinking it's something you have to perform. You could spend your entire life doing that and never know any more of Me at all. You'll miss the point, miss the beauty, and miss the sky I painted above you.

It's a beautiful night to realize what it's really like to be loved.

Stop chasing the song, child, and let Me teach you to sing.

CHAPTER 1

Monday

Ultimately the man who comes to obey God will love Him first . . .
Let us therefore learn that the love of God is the beginning of religion,
for God will not have the forced obedience of men,
but wishes their service to be free and spontaneous . . .
Lastly we learn that God does not linger over the outward sign of
achievement but chiefly searches the inner disposition [motive],
that from a good root good fruits may grow.

~ JOHN CALVIN

W e lived at the top of a winding hill, and from the balcony off my bedroom I could see a good part of the city. Especially at night, when it was all lights and silence except for the occasional plane flying overhead.

I would stand with my toes between the metal bars and look down the streets and then out at the water in the distance. I would imagine that I was part of a grand adventure, and that my life was encapsulated in an epic story. It felt better than loneliness.

The truth was that none of the people in the houses I could see knew my name and they didn't speak the language I spoke. We were strangers in a foreign country, doing our best to blend into the Japanese culture with our bright red hair and awkward accents.

Our apartment building had only three floors, with one family on each. We were in the middle, right below Yenny and her family and right above another European family who we befriended mostly because their video game selection overshadowed their attitudes. We would play Lode Runner on the "Family Entertainment System" until my mother would phone down and tell us supper was ready. Aside from those two families, there was no one who spoke English within walking distance. During the daylight hours you could hear all the laughter and chatter of families while they strung up laundry and watched their kids play. They would nod and wave, and we would do the same, but we didn't know each other's names.

We bowed our heads and smiled, but we didn't share life.

So much kindness, but still a deep sense of "not belonging," and always wondering what everyone thought of the little American girls who stared off the balcony.

But Yenny was very nice. And I liked to go up to her floor on weekends when her parents would make pancakes and we would play "orphans" and hide under her bed. She had a lot more imagination than she did toys, and she was perfectly content with that.

On Christmas morning one year, I called her up to ask her what Santa had brought her. She explained that she had gotten a few good gifts and one "really special one."

I was expecting a new tape deck or "Teddy Ruxpin," but as soon as I asked her what it was, she said excitedly, "A BIBLE!"

I wrapped things up with her and hung up the phone, explaining to my family that evidently Yenny hadn't acted right this year because Santa had basically forgotten her.

My sister asked what she got, and I told her.

She shook her head sadly from side to side.

"That's it? A Bible? Awful . . ."

"I know." I replied solemnly. "And she seems like such a good kid."

"Was she crying?" Jennifer asked.

"No." I shook my head, incredulous at the reality. "She was *excited.*"

"Well don't tell her about our Cabbage Patch dolls."

"I won't. It'll be too much right now."

Later that night Yenny asked me to come up so we could show each other our gifts. I brought a board game and some candy from my stocking because there was no need to pour salt in the wound of her punishment. I mean, clearly Santa did love me the most, but I didn't want her to get all upset. There's always next year, you know?

"Come on in!" Her mother smiled, the door open wide. Yenny stood behind her and motioned for me to come in as she darted down the hallway to her room.

She asked me about my loot and I laid it out cautiously, downplaying the abundance of stuff I had left at home.

I cleared my throat.

"And what about you? You said you got some chocolate, right? And a, umm, a Bible?"

Her face lit up.

I can see her now, sitting with her back to the window and the city sparkling down below as she reached under her bed and pulled out a box with her name on it.

The wrapping was torn, but still covered a good bit of the gift, so I could tell she had saved every bit of it. I thought about the way we tore through ours like a hurricane, filling black trash bags and grabbing at whatever was left with our names on it.

She slid it out and opened the box, revealing a hardback Bible with images of different characters on the cover. She smiled and handed it to me. "Isn't it beautiful?"

It was beautiful. I mean, as beautiful as a Bible could be. Which was obviously not as beautiful as a doll that told you when she needed to nap and eat. But still, I wanted to be encouraging.

I opened the pages and scanned the stories, asking her to tell me what some of them were about. She obliged willingly, all the while reminding me it was the first one that was just hers.

I handed it back to her and watched her leaf through the pages slowly, taking it in again. I knew in that moment that Yenny didn't think she had gotten the short end of the stick.

And I also started to realize she saw her gift as more than a pretty storybook.

After a few minutes she tucked it back in the box and we played the way we always did, but I was distracted by the memory of her staring at the words with life on her face. I wondered what she saw there, and why it made her so happy.

It was the first experience I can recall having with the Bible.

A little girl in a big city, clinging to the few people that God had put in her midst.

I wish I could go back for a moment and watch that little girl climb down the twenty-two stairs to her apartment after hugging her friend good-bye. I wish I could see her slide open the balcony door as she did every other night, but this time having a new question for the night.

"What makes her love that book?"

Because the truth of the matter is that the little red-headed girl would grow to be a woman who loved the same Lord, and who treasured His Word like the finest gift under any Christmas tree. And there's a part of me that would long to whisper to her as she looked as far as her eyes could see—to tell her all that she could see and all she would ever know in this great life was breathed by the One who spoke the words in the book just one floor above her.

And maybe she would know, even then, that the nights and the languages and the loneliness and misunderstandings were for her good. They would teach her things she would rely on later.

I would also tell her that the planes she counted every night carried people all over the world, and that one day she would take her seat on many of them. She would have cried from fear, but I would reassure her.

One day you'll know why she wrapped it up that way, and you will understand the tenderness of the pages turning. You'll find the refuge you've tried to create for yourself.

And one day, many years from now, He will be Your hope.

She would have seen the city differently—not just as a child, but for years to come.

I know the curiosity that burned in her, and it was only recently that I felt it again. I was taller, though not much, and my toes pressed into wet sand while waves kissed my feet and tugged me forward over and over.

I wasn't playing games about being an orphan or trying to beat a high score, but I was still on the second floor pretending instead of allowing the reality of God to be bigger than the dreaming of Him.

I was acting like a Christian, doing things Christians did, and generally succeeding at being "A Christian." At least, on paper.

But my fingers didn't cling to the words the way hers did, and a good part of my mind wondered things I was scared to even say out loud. *What if none of this is real? What if I'm not doing it right? What is it that makes faith look more like a treasured gift than a consolation prize? What makes this dance feel true to my spirit, and where do I look for the answers?*

Others have met Him; they've been in His presence. They've been consumed by His love for them, and I don't know how.

It's not for lack of trying, either. If chasing God was an Olympic sport, I feel certain I would be on a Wheaties box within a matter of months. Effort. More effort. Doing. More doing. Trying. A little more trying. Have I mentioned trying? Okay, good.

Despite that, I hadn't grown closer to Him because I had a faulty understanding of my role and His. Truth be told, it's a pattern that would have continued were it not for the answer that came to me in a moment of desperation.

How do I find You, Lord?

I didn't hear His voice audibly, but I understood what He was saying and it rattled me deeply. Three words that would change my entire approach to Christianity, and would allow me to be His in the way He always intended for me to be.

Stop.

Chasing.

Me.

I didn't know for a long while what that meant or what it would look like, but I knew He had given me a song, and for the first time in my walk, I was more concerned with singing than I was the people who passed the harp around.

What seemed at first to be a case of semantics quickly proved to be the key that unlocked my faith.

We aren't supposed to chase Him.

The parts of our walk that feel like a hunt are the areas where we've confused man's idea of God with God Himself.

They're the places where we've looked at the wrong measuring tool to tell us how we're doing, and then promote frustration and the sense that we're way behind the pack.

We're going to unpack this in the coming chapters, and I'm going to encourage you to just let the Lord speak as you read, showing you the ways you may have convinced yourself to pursue God without God actually asking you to do so. It's a new way of thinking about the journey, and in order to begin, we have to go all the way back to the start and see where we've allowed skewed interpretations to send us running after what we perceive to be the right goal.

Even the very concept of "salvation" might be a little muddy to many of us, so it's good to just take a step back and study what Scripture says about it. Maybe you're nothing like me in this area, but honestly, I didn't really get it at all. It felt a bit like a club where I had to learn a secret handshake and a password, and I was so confused about why that was the way the God of the universe had set things up.

I realized that even from the very beginning of my Christian life I was doing things that I thought I was supposed to, yet they weren't reassuring me or making me feel like I was a "member."

Trust me. By the end of this book, you'll understand how VERY confused I was about all the "Christianese," and how pitiful my attempts were to look like the rest of the bunch. But when I felt the Lord urging me to write this book, it was because I really understood what it was like to long for Him but not know Him.

And maybe (Maybe? Please?) you've wondered some of the same things.

He's God. Not a formula.

This book was inspired by my own bumbling attempts to understand what the Christian walk looked like. I was so concerned with fulfilling the *requirements* that I missed the heart of the gospel.

In other words, I used religion to fill in the gaps of my faith.

I was too tangled in the details to recognize the point, and it wasn't the way He intended our relationship to be.

Let's sit with the Word and ask the Lord to give us a fresh glimpse of His calling on our lives. And while we're at the beginning, let's also make a little commitment to each other. This isn't about denominations or legalism, it's about a genuine desire to know, understand, and obey the Bible. You might not agree with everything I'm going to present to you, and that's okay. You're allowed to be wrong.

Do tell me you're giggling and not grabbing that last paragraph to post online, completely out of context.

Because to take one sentence out of context and run with it would be irresponsible, wouldn't you agree? It renders the big picture irrelevant, and pits us against things we don't even have exposure to.

I've done it myself many times.

And so have you.

In fact (caution: sweeping, bold-worthy statement is about to be made), I think the church has done a pretty good job of taking things out of context at times. We love to quote verses but we don't necessarily know where or how they fit into the grand scheme of God's Word. We pick and choose and print them on our children's bedroom walls, but we can't say we've ever read that particular book of the Bible.

Obviously this is a huge generalization, but I've found myself doing this at times. Desiring truth but not really feeling like it's possible to attain it for myself. Yes, I can physically read the Bible, but how in the world am I supposed to understand what it says? There are smart people who can draw me pictures, right?

I'm asking the Lord to speak to you as you read. I hope the process of learning more about the true heart of God will bless you the way it has me, and I'm eager to walk alongside you in what I hope will be a fresh start in your faith.

With that said, I'm well aware that there's a lot of potential for confusion and questioning as we explore together what it means to have a relationship with God, so here's the heads-up before we start working our way through it all.

I don't have all the answers.

God does.

He gave us some of them.

Those are the ones we need to spend our lives studying.

The rest are for Him to reveal when He chooses, if at all.

But He has given us what we need to rest and we should not be nearly as unsettled in the mystery as we are settled in the promises.

Here are three words you are going to have to get used to saying if you're going to follow Jesus: *I don't know.*

I realize that's uncomfortable. In a few paragraphs, you'll see I'm the one who knocked everyone else down to get to the front of the "I need more information" line.

I'm seriously obsessed with checklists and the feeling of accomplishment and completion. I'm relatively intelligent according to standardized testing, and I think diagramming sentences is fun. I read a lot of books written by dead people (they were not in that state when said books were written), and I hold a Master's degree in developmental psychology.

In addition, I can solve the puzzle before the *Wheel of Fortune* contestants at least 60 percent of the time.

I'm a thinker. A learner. An evaluator.

In other words, I'm a likely candidate to chase God.

I'm one of those people who want to wrestle it to the ground until it submits in all its clarity. If I were being honest with you, I would say that I'm surprised I've ended up where I have with a God who leaves so much gray.

Ultimately, what I found was that the gray only hovers in the secondary issues, and I can live with that because what matters is in solid black and white.

But it wasn't always this way; in fact, up until the last several years I was doing a much better job imitating other Christians than I was God, and it wasn't working.

I read a lot of books about spiritual disciplines and I decided I was going to live them out as best I could. I tried to be creative with it because I didn't want to be one of those boring rule-keepers, so I bought leather-bound journals and colorful markers. I made lists of behaviors I wanted to change, complete with Bible verses expounding on the reasoning.

I would pick a virtue for the day and focus on living it out. At the end of the day I would write down my successes and failures, and would make a plan for how to do better the next day. I know what you're thinking, and I assure you I had the same question.

How could this possibly go wrong?

(Note: Reader, meet sarcasm. She is a friend of mine, and she likes to jump in periodically. I hope you'll love her like I do.)

It was an intense amount of work, that's for sure. But it wasn't getting me anywhere. Still, I kept at it because I was sure I just hadn't found the right method.

Maybe it was the fact that I didn't have post-it notes with Bible verses on my mirror. Could be because I listened to secular radio on the way to work. Noted.

Tuesday will be better, I kept telling myself.

But Tuesday never came.

My faith was a perpetual Monday.

Get filled up at church on Sunday, figure out how to try and apply what I learned to my own life, and then spend a full day failing. *Really? This is the goal?* Because it feels like prison.

A prison I could escape from if only I could find the right key . . . *surely there's a way . . .*

In case you haven't picked up on this, I'm what you might call "determined." Or at least I like to say it that way because it sounds much more lovable than it's abrasive synonyms, "stubborn" and "prideful."

I would scribble notes to myself during church because half the time I didn't understand what the lesson was about and I knew I needed to do some digging in my own time.

I laughed when the congregation laughed, and I nodded when they nodded. I wanted to be like God, and I figured they were what that looked like in the flesh.

My motives weren't bad; they just weren't *right*.

Just tell me what I need to do, here, and I'll do my best.

More post-its, more nodding, and more Mondays.

A lot of Christians live this way, but not a lot will say so because it means they are risking their status as good students.

Which, unfortunately, is the heart of the problem.

If I'm just trying to do as well as the other kids, I'm comparing myself to the wrong source. If I'm using knowledge as my gauge of righteousness, either end of the continuum I'm on will result in wrong thinking about God. I'm either too ignorant to ever be used or so convinced of my own knowledge that I ignore the lecture.

While I called Him teacher, I looked to the other students to tell me how I was faring in the school of faith.

I was exhausted. I felt like a failure. I just flat-out felt like I had missed the part where they handed out the manual.

Over a period of time, I realized I had neglected the basic truths He had given as His standards in favor of a system that looked more manageable. It was no longer enough for me to "get by," and I knew that in order to really follow God I would have to do something I hadn't even considered a viable option.

So I opened the Book I had tucked behind all the commentaries, and I told Him I wanted to know who He was.

As I discovered, this is not a request He turns down.

And as I also discovered, there is no going back once you ask.

———————————

The truth is that our journey with God isn't really about living, and He never claimed it would be. It is, and has always been, a gradual death to everything we love outside of Him.

For obvious reasons, this has yet to become a bumper sticker craze.

We don't want to feel like it's going to be difficult, so we package it up in slogans and self-help lingo and we call it Christianity. We carefully scoot emphasis to the "overcoming" verses and dodge the bullets that might make us look like a bunch of lunatics who are willingly embracing a doctrine grounded in humility and suffering. Solid theology and good marketing strategies don't necessarily go hand in hand. Which is why this tweet never happens:

"Come to the retreat on Saturday if you can; we're doing skits on depravity and desperation! #GoGod!!"

And listen, I'm not suggesting we turn all gloom and doom, because that would be missing the point as well. What I do want to encourage is an approach to your Christian walk that is based more on Scripture than an emotional high or stellar sermon series.

Don't worry.

This isn't a pounding-my-fists-and-getting-red-faced chapter. I don't ever pound my fists and I only get red-faced when I fall in public. Hypothetically, of course.

In fact, this chapter is quite the opposite. It's a conversation between you and a girl who realized she was wrong about what "following God" looked like. And she's not angry. She's grateful to have found the peace she spent so many years searching for. And she's still speaking in the third person, which is somewhat odd. Two sentences? Off-putting. Three? Borderline narcissistic.

I broke up with a guy once because he slipped into third person like it was a pair of cozy flannel pajamas. To that I say, *"No sir."*

And here's the part where I move from "nutty ex" to "you need Jesus." Let's call that transition what it is, folks: *seamless.*

Truly, though, we will never know God without first recognizing our need for Him. I hasten to say the larger the gap between what He *actually* did for you and what you *believe* He did for you, the more likely you are to continue chasing Him.

At least when you're chasing Him you still have some sense of control, right? Yeah. I know. I have the post-its to prove it.

So let's make sure we're clear on what the Bible actually says is required in order for you to be a true believer of Christ.

That last sentence? Number 3,412,543,768 on the list of things I felt I might write about one day. I have to believe the Lord is enjoying the fact that I'm intermittently squirming and finding things to deep clean around my house in-between paragraphs.

My husband was already supportive of my writing, but he's even more-so now that he can see his reflection in the kitchen sink and use the color-coded diagram in the closet to locate his socks.

Let's just say this isn't my comfort zone.

I assure you, you're in good (and remarkably clean) hands.

I want to share what I understand to be the path on which God has called us to walk, but I have to acknowledge that not all of us are at the same stage of that walk. To some of you, it's going to look like I'm trying to rack up scrabble points, and for others of you it will be a yawn-worthy, simplistic explanation of concepts you were teaching in a foreign language before you could write your name. I get it. And I want you to know up-front that I'm aware of issues and have taken some precautionary steps in order to serve my audience.

Because it was important to me that I was seen as approachable, I decided to write this manuscript in English instead of what comes more naturally to me—the ancient Hebrew and Greek. So in the instances where it seems to you scholars that I am presenting the equivalent of a glorified Sunday school lesson, I need you to know it was a *choice*.

If you're interested in e-mailing me about the Hebrew/ Greek transcripts, I will include my assistant's information at the end of this chapter and you can contact her. She's very responsible so I assume you should receive a copy sometime between now and not ever.

New kids, *you're welcome.*

Now find a seat on the rug while I tuck my expositional-commentary-parallel-reference stuff away real quick.

(Note: If you don't appreciate a little humor in the midst of critically important theological issues, you may not have come to the same conclusion I have, which is this: I don't have to take myself too seriously in order to take God seriously.)

Okay. Let's go.

At its most basic level, a person is saved by the grace of God through the acknowledgment that he or she is a sinner who cannot earn God's favor, but is trusting in the sacrifice of Jesus to pay for his or her sins.

The moment you profess this is also referred to as "justification." Feel free to throw that around your next Bible study meeting.

Bonus points if you use the catchphrase, "It's just as if you never sinned." I don't take credit for it but I do think it's clever, and one of my favorite teachers used it once so I'm just passing along the goodness.

Justification is a big word with even bigger implications for our lives. Why? What does that mean? Two thousand years ago, Jesus took the form of a man in order to be crucified on our behalf. When He died, He took with Him all the sins we've committed and have yet to commit, and His perfection was accepted in place of our imperfection. It's what allows us access to Him, and without acknowledging it, we're lost.

Don't skim this because you've seen it all before. It's not a boring lecture. And if you're someone (as I am) who starts to tune out anything that sounds more like a pitch than a promise, trust me. I get it. I've been there, done that.

I'm not trying to sell you something here.

I'm reminding you that you've been *bought*.

Wherever you are, whatever you're doing—stop, breathe for a minute, and put aside anything negative that you carry with you about being saved, faith, the Bible, or God. Just until I finish, okay?

We can never take the cross for granted.

When we nod our heads and our hearts remain unmoved, we've taken it for granted. Our pride has shadowed the power of Calvary in our lives, and we are willfully allowing it to continue.

I know that sounds harsh, but it has to because truth doesn't always have soft edges.

With that said, I'm going to ask you to do me a favor before we go much farther.

I want you to remove the image you have of someone behind a pulpit, shouting about what you really deserve, spewing fear and condemnation while repeating the word *hell* over and over in increasing intensity.

Because I saw that happen on an episode of *Little House on the Prairie* once when I was a kid, and it's a miracle I ever set foot in a church again.

Or a barn. Or a general store for that matter.

And forget a school for the blind. The word *braille* sends shivers down my spine and I can almost hear Mary's blood-curdling screams in the middle of the night. I'm still not convinced that story line was worth the hours of therapy incurred as a result. There were a lot of those moments, looking back. Hey Ingalls? *I was nine.* I needed a good hair-braiding/dress-sewing episode, not the dead-eyed gypsy guy who comes to town peddling his freaky ware.

I'm over-sharing.

I can see that now.

What I'm saying is that we do a disservice to the kingdom of God when we present Him this way. When we are so caught up in hammering people into obeying just because they're too afraid to consider the alternative. And I'm pretty convinced that it's not an approach that's going to lead to a life dedicated to Jesus.

My job is not to scare you into doing what God tells you to do. And when people try to introduce you to Jesus with more threats than promises, there is reason to believe they haven't fully gotten their theology straight.

For the record, I do fear God. *A lot.*

But it's sure not because someone told me I had to.

I fear Him because I am overwhelmed by His love and I see no other option.

The fact of the matter is that if we were able to feel the full weight of what God had done for us, we wouldn't be shouting from pulpits.

In fact, we wouldn't be standing at all.

We would be face-down on the ground in worship, so consumed with the gracious, life-giving love of a Savior that we could scarcely catch our breath in the first place.

So for the rest of this book, I want you to tuck that image of an angry preacher away. It's impossible to embrace the one true God unless you know what underlies every single command in the Bible.

Pure and perfect love.

Not judgment. Not hatred. Not cruelty. Not a desire to punish us.

Love.

You might not be looking at this as anything new, and really, it isn't. But that doesn't mean you believe it the way you should.

You've probably heard it your entire life. God is love, God is love . . . where are we going for lunch?

So often, we sweep mercy under the rug of legalism, and in the process we bind up what was meant to free us.

We rely on the wrong things to make it all right, and they never will.

We exhaust ourselves with our own images of Him, and I don't necessarily think our intentions are always wrong. We can't comprehend the truth in all it's wild simplicity, so we create a version of Christianity that appeals more to our sensibilities.

We spend more time arguing about God than we do experiencing Him.

We want to make our points, make up our minds, make our own decisions.

We would sooner shake the tree than eat the fruit we've been given, because it gives us a sense of ownership.

I'm afraid there are areas where we've allowed our desire for clarification to outshine biblical explanations. Salvation is simply too important a concept to allow misunderstanding, so I'm going to spend just a little time on where I think there's room for confusion, and then I'm going to tie up the chapter with an air-tight explanation of propitiation.

That last sentence isn't "definitely" going to happen. I'll just play it by ear depending on how y'all are feeling after snack time.

People refer to salvation in a lot of different ways. Some say they "accepted Jesus," or "got saved." Others refer to it as when they "asked Jesus into their heart," or "made Him their personal Savior." I'm going to be straight with you here, because we're on our second date (section, topic . . . whatever. We're in this thing together now, right?). There are a few things in this paragraph that make me itchy, and I'd feel better if we could talk it out a bit.

The first is that the phrase "ask Jesus into your heart" is not in the Bible. Like, at all.

There's also not an example given at any point in the Bible where someone repeats what is often called "the sinners prayer" in response to realizing their need for God. They don't do a "repeat after me" thing. Not once.

I'm not kidding. Did you know that already? Well, good for you if you did. Because that little tidbit of information would have come in handy in every one of the fourteen million times I acted like that was my J.O.B. in order to get into heaven.

Maybe I'm the only person who thought this whole "Say what I say" thing was standard protocol for getting right with God. But it stressed me out a lot, because what if I said the prayer in the wrong order? What if I missed a key word?

Believing that your vocabulary solidifies your eternal standing is quite a bit of pressure, no?

If our lives were movies we could just stop and replay however we wanted, I would make a little video to include with this book. It would be a series of clips featuring me reciting different versions of the "sinner's prayer" at various points in the last ten years or so. There would be emo-ish music playing softly in the background to enhance dramatic effect. I'm just saying, it could work. I might see if there's a movie studio interested and also confirm that my doppelgänger Blake Lively is available before I proceed.

A couple scenes might feature me bowing my head in church, others might be me lying in bed in the middle of the night because I can't fall asleep until I know I'm in the clear, and more than a few would occur as my plane is taking off. Evidently runways inspire me to "recommit."

"Are we good? Did I do it right? I mean, You would tell me, right? Because sometimes I just wonder. So I'm going to go through the motions again to make sure it's settled."

For the record, it would be a very long video and Blangie would cry a lot.

Also for the record, *recommit* or *rededicate* isn't a biblical term either. Yeah. I know. I'm taking the T-shirt back ASAP.

When you feel like you have to keep "trying to get saved," you're *chasing God.*

Salvation isn't about sets of words. It's an attitude of the heart. The words have no power in and of themselves; it's not a formula we have to perfect in order to be accepted.

So if you're worried you might not be saved because you didn't "do it correctly," I have good news and bad news. It's actually the same news, but depending on how tightly you're gripping the belief that you can save yourself, you'll hear it more one way than the other. If we're worried about our part, the underlying issue is that we have a misappropriated sense of our own ability. The notion that our words could allow us access to God hinges on a principal that is wholly refuted throughout Scripture—that we have the power to save.

We don't.

On several occasions, I have seen the gospel presented as something not unlike a carnival ticket. You say the words, you get the ticket, and you ride the ride. It felt a little weird, but who was I to question God?

It wasn't until later that I realized I wasn't questioning God, but I had some serious reservations about a couple of the sellers. They were most likely the ones who were ripping tickets up at the end of the night and "praising God" for all the new converts they had brought to Christ.

In other words, they felt good about being a part of something as big as God, but they didn't realize He was so big that they couldn't be good if they tried.

I call this "trying to sell God," and it's faulty on a number of levels, including the fact that I could have at least come up with a snazzier title for such a huge concept.

To begin with, we don't hold those tickets. We don't open the door to heaven and let people in. We don't stamp hands or ask for more money. We don't threaten people if they don't do it our way, and we don't have a say in other people's eternal standing. Period. God can use our mouths to speak His words, but the credit doesn't go to us, it goes to Him.

We live in skin that loves applause, and we often bow to crowds that never saw us at all. Don't mistake being *used* by God for being *necessary* to God.

He is not waiting for you to make things right and do your part so the universe doesn't split in half.

In addition to the fact that we don't distribute "eternal wristbands," it is wildly irresponsible to give someone the impression that they can buy a ticket with their words.

A gospel that comes to me courtesy of my own willpower is not the gospel at all.

Do I have a role in the exchange? Sure I do. And it's not an insignificant one. The error is in believing we caused it, or that we ponied up to the counter with something to offer in order to make it a fair exchange. It is the free gift of God.

It doesn't matter what you say or do or feel or want or dream or imagine your role was. The reality is that He did the beautiful thing you could never do. He chose us in spite of ourselves, and without that, we would never have found Him.

Get it right out of your head that there is something you can do so right that you'll "earn God." You won't. You can't. Ever.

"No one can come to me unless the Father who sent me draws him" (John 6:44).

And it also leads me to believe that there are many people who, despite being professing Christians, are not actually saved.

Jesus warns His disciples about this as He explains, "Not everyone who says to me, 'Lord, Lord,' will enter the kingdom of heaven, but only who does the will of my Father who is in heaven" (Matt. 7:21).

God doesn't want us to be unsure of our salvation, but I also believe He warns us against believing we are saved because we repeated a couple words one time in a church service.

The best we can do is to accept His gracious offer, walking where His mercy has led. If we start out our journey with Christ with the impression that we were responsible for our own salvation, we've shifted the weight in the wrong direction.

Let us begin by remembering the sacrifice that made the steps ahead of us possible. With praise on our lips and conviction in our hearts, let us recognize the King as we set one foot in front of the other in response to His gracious love for us.

CHAPTER 2

Called

But here the doubter may say, "Ah yes, this is no doubt
all true, but how can I get ahold of it?
I am such a poor, unworthy creature that I dare
not believe such a fullness of grace can belong to me."
How can you get ahold of it, you ask.

You cannot get hold of it at all,
but you can let it get hold of you.

~ HANNAH WHITALL SMITH

I started writing when I was old enough to know what that
meant. It was the only way I could make what was in my
head make sense. It was my own little therapy, and it almost
always involved a canopy bed and lamenting whatever wrong
I felt like I was a victim of that day.

Not always, though.

I do recall writing a rather inspired piece about starlight and a lonely pixie, but it never sorted itself out. Starlight is so ambiguous, isn't it? And you can't rely on the pixies for anything.

I realized early on that I didn't like the subjects that couldn't be nailed down and molded into predictable, tangible sentences. Fantasy wasn't that interesting to me because there were too many variables. And also, pixie is a pain to rhyme. If you're like me, you just said the word "Dixie" and considered it moderately successful. It doesn't lead to the Pulitzer, I can assure you.

Instead, what interested me the most was the way my sister blew bubbles or the feeling of rain on my shoulders. Things that were interesting, yes, but also real. I loved describing the everyday things that other people might not notice.

I did take a sharp departure in the sixth grade by penning a series about talking animals that lived in a haunted motel, but really, who hasn't? It's the writer's equivalent to Journey's "Faithfully." It just feels right.

I was "published" in a school newspaper at the ripe age of eight, when I wrote a stirring poem about helping poor people in Africa. It took me at least thirty minutes to write, which signified unparalleled devotion at that point in life.

It ended with this power punch: "We should give, so they can live."

I'm not going to say it isn't genius, because clearly nobody in the history of the world has thought to rhyme these words in such a powerful closing line. Who are we kidding? I was destined for greatness.

There was a buzz around the school when it came out (and by "buzz," I mean a couple people saw my name in the paper. One even took the time to tell me I had an unfortunate last name for publication, which, as you can imagine, really blessed me).

My dad got several copies to have at the house. You know, in case company came over. It's always good to have evidence that you're raising people who can link four-letter words with such gusto.

What I love about my dad is that he can encourage and critique in the same breath, and it has a way of making you feel like they come from the same well of love. If there was criticism, it wasn't for the sake of hurting but rather because he wanted me to get better. I remember reading him a poem one night and having him tell me that I shouldn't just put those words in because they sounded pretty, and that I needed to make sure I was saying something that mattered to me.

I still hear that voice, even as my fingers jump from letter to letter on the keyboard. "Pay attention to why you're doing this. And if it's just to make something look pretty and get your name in a school paper, you should close up shop for now and wait until you're writing because you're too moved not to write it."

Not that he ever said that exact sentence, but it's underneath the sentiments he wanted me to embrace, even as a kid.

Your motivation matters.

I did get some attention from the Africa poem, but it bounced off of me because I knew anyone with an hour and a decent thesaurus could give me a run for my money. It wasn't really something I had poured out, but rather something I just presented because it fit within the guidelines of "good writing."

I evaluated what a poem should look like and then I went through the motions of creating one. It wasn't that it was bad, but it wasn't what it could be.

He saw that, I guess, and he wanted more from me.

I wrote a lot more frequently after that but most of it was inconsequential. A glorified journal of thoughts and observations. I completed my writing assignments based on what the rules were, and I did just fine.

There was an assignment given to my class sometime later in the year, and for whatever reason, I started feeling something different as I worked on it. I really cared about it. I didn't just lay the words down; I searched for them. I chased them until they fit like puzzle pieces. It was a treasure hunt, and I loved every minute. I don't remember a lot of details, but I know it mentioned a baby's eyelashes.

I can sense you're on the edge of your seat with curiosity.

In retrospect it might have actually been as trite as my other "works" on paper.

The difference was that it was born from a true place in me, a distinction that has ultimately led to writing this book. I'll explain more about that, but for now, just know that it's always been a source of struggle in my life, whether in writing or just plain conversation over coffee with a friend.

The quality of the work might not have been much different to the average eye, but I had a great teacher that year, the kind that notices the areas of life that need speaking into and is honored to be that voice.

She was returning our papers, and mine landed on my desk like all the others had, with marks indicating that I had done the work. Basically, I had remembered my capital letters and ending punctuation, so I received the coveted 2-word acceptance phrase: "Well done."

I didn't think any more of it, but as she walked past me again, she paused and knelt down by my desk, eye-to-eye. She tapped my paper with her finger and smiled, quietly making a declaration that breathed purpose into me.

"You, my dear, were born to be a writer."

She gave my hand a little squeeze and continued returning papers like nothing had happened. She had whispered it so that nobody else could hear, and as I watched her move around the classroom, it felt like a delicious secret.

What did she see that day? I won't ever know for sure.

It was still the same messy, half-filled, imperfect page I had turned in a few days earlier, but there was suddenly a seed of potential that felt worthy of growing.

That's what great teachers do, you know.

They remind you that what you've done is nothing in comparison to what you are called to do, and they plant a seed that will grow in spite of it.

What would have been subtle to most people wasn't lost on her. It was beautiful and praiseworthy not because I had performed a task, but rather because I let it pour out of the deepest sense of truth I could grasp at that point. It was work inspired by love, not by report cards and the admiration of others.

Motivation.

Like I said, it matters.

I didn't leave school and write my debut novella that day. I can't even tell you with certainty that I remember her name. I do know this, though. That sentence has played over and over in my mind on days when I'm staring at a screen and wondering how in the world I'm going to fill it with words. It has been a source of confidence to me when I can't see it in myself.

And you know what? I might not ever be an award-winning (or even a great) writer, but she made me *want* to be, if for no other reason than to thank her for the gift she gave me. She told me I was born to write, and that was the beginning of a journey for me.

I didn't do anything spectacular right away and I didn't focus too much on what it might look like down the road. What I did do was what anyone would do when an English teacher told her she was a writer. I picked up my pencil and turned to a new page.

And when I did, I noticed I was holding it a little bit differently than I ever had before.

In the first chapter of John, we learn that John had met the Lord and had recognized Him as the Son of God. In verse 35, we see John standing with two other men, Andrew and Simon Peter. Jesus walked by, and John immediately declared, "Behold, the Lamb of God!"

It's possible that John had been telling them all about His experience with Jesus the previous day, revealing that he had seen the Spirit descend like a dove on the Lord. His heart had no doubt been stirred and I imagine him passionately telling them that he believed he had met the true God. When John pointed Jesus out, the men were all too anxious to follow Him themselves. I love the fact that Scripture doesn't mention them asking Him anything, nor even greeting Him. It's as if they were so moved by His presence that they simply started *walking*.

That's the first important thing we can do as disciples of Christ. No big questions, no interrogations, no agenda. Just our steps, one after another, as we seek to walk the road His feet are carving.

Don't worry. He won't leave things silent for long.

"What are you seeking?" Jesus asks them when He sees them following (John 1:38).

In other words, "What are you hoping to gain here? What do you want from Me?" It isn't a rebuke, but rather a question posed in love and interest.

Imagine the scene; they have started walking behind Him and He turns to them to ask what it is they desire.

What a beautiful image of our Lord, ever loving and wanting us to know we are valuable to Him. We walk and He turns to us. What a gift it is to serve a God so interested in the personal details.

They answer Him with a question of their own.

"Rabbi, where are you staying?"

Well, that didn't really tell Jesus what they were seeking, did it? Actually, if we dig a little deeper we will see that it just might. The term *rabbi* means several things, most notably, "teacher." So right away they are acknowledging that He has some authority, even though they have yet to even be introduced to Him. The fact that they asked where He was staying isn't to dodge His question. It was likely to tell Him they were interested in going with Him, but they weren't being presumptuous that He would allow them to do so. In one brief sentence, the first we hear the disciples speak, they give two references to the fact that they look up to Him and, in a sense, defer to Him.

I see a lot of myself here, eager to follow but desiring a little more information about the plan. I really want to just go along with things, but more often than not I end up digging for some clarity on what's coming up next. I'm not saying the first disciples had my control freak tendencies, but I can totally see myself casually walking and trying to work in a little hint that I'd sure love to know what was on the old agenda.

"Angie, what do you want?"

"Oh, me? I want to follow You wherever You go. Whatever comes next. I'm game for the adventure and no matter what, I'll be right behind You. I'm just happy to be here, Lord."

I somehow make it five more steps in silence.

"The landscape is pretty here. Feels like we might be headed north . . . is it north, Lord? I mean, I'm good with it even if it's east, but I'm thinking it's north. Am I right? I wonder if we'll pass any good lunch spots on the way. I'm not starving, but I can tell I might get hungry in a bit . . ."

I'm going out on a limb here and guessing I'm not the only one who might do this, which is why I find His answer so appropriate (and yet, uninformative as far as a calendar or map is concerned).

"Come and you will see."

So few words, and yet so profoundly important to incorporate into our own understanding of God. It sets up the journey so succinctly and identifies our roles as we go. We aren't to be passive about it, but instead, we are to take action. What kind of action? Let's look at these words before we go on.

In Scripture, the word *chase* (*radaph*) means "to aim to secure."[1] In other words, we have a preconceived notion of "arriving" that includes our ability to maintain a sense of control once we get there.

Contrast that with the word for *follow* (*akoloutheō*), which means "to accompany; to cleave steadfastly to one, conforming wholly to his example, in living and if need be, in dying."[2]

It is effort to be sure, but not in order to "secure" and arrive. It is the sweat that comes from making His example our highest calling, constantly aware of our need for His grace in the process. It's not saying we are the ones in charge of finding Him, but rather, our goal is to walk in a way that makes us more like Him every day.

It's easy to see, even here from the outset, that our natural tendency would be to ask, *"How? What does that mean? How do I know if I'm walking the right way?"*

There's a part of me (and it's not minute) that would love for Him to have handed a syllabus over to them, highlighting the parts for which they might want to be prepared. Or, at the very least, that wishes He would have given them a word of encouragement that they were making the right choice.

"I know you don't really understand who I am, but trust Me. You're going to be glad you did this. I'm going to turn the world upside-down and I'm giving you a front-row seat. Ready?"

And yes, I realize this isn't always possible, but He's God. Certainly He can manage a little bullet-point pamphlet every now and then.

It's not a coincidence that He doesn't often do so; not for them and not for us. It's one of the beautiful (and challenging) things about the God who invites us to be a part of His story. He gives us what we need even when we don't feel like it's enough, and our acceptance is good practice in surrender.

He is leading and you are following. It's His map, His road, and His time line.

I can't help but wince just a little here, because I thrive on predictability and, as my mother would say, a decent "fountain coke."

We would be on a road trip somewhere and she would wait until the car was silent and then in a hushed, "I didn't realize I was speaking out loud" tone, she would say, "Well, I'll be. What I wouldn't give for a fountain coke right about now."

It's important to hear this in your head the way it actually came out, which was laced with her Charlotte, North Carolinian roots. "I" sounds harsh, but "Ahhh" is so unassuming and gentle, no? And while "give" might look like a one syllable word on paper, her mouth considered that an insult. Why not make it three? "Geh-ye-vuh."

My sister and I could reliably count no higher than thirty before the blinker was on and the station wagon was taking a detour to the nearest drive-thru.

Passive aggressive? Sure, I guess you could say that. But she would much prefer you realize she had not demanded her way, but rather made a comment that was taken as an opportunity to bless her. She's Southern, you realize, and it's not ladylike to tell someone to pull the car over. It could even be perceived as selfish ("Ahhh woooood *neavaahhh* . . .") or bossy, so it's preferable to opt for talking out loud to yourself.

We teased her mercilessly about the fountain coke, as well as ten million other things she could work into any situation to benefit her. It was a gift, really. A gift that I saw as useless in life, and ridiculous at best.

It was really much funnier before I got married. But I digress.

When we agree to go along with the Lord, we do get something better than a Big Gulp in return, and He tells us up front what we can expect.

At first glance you might think it isn't much, but it's actually pretty amazing. It's a promise that we will cling to many times as we go.

"You will see."

Walk, love. And all of the glory will go to the God who allows your feet to follow Mine.

It won't be for nothing. It might feel like blind faith sometimes, but ultimately you will see it with your own eyes in a way that words can't convey. I want you to be a part of the story, and the only way to do that is to have you walk it yourself.

The original language used in this text suggests more than seeing with one's eyes, and indicates "becoming acquainted by experience."[3]

Am I the only one that struggles with not fully (or remotely) understanding and living out of the truth He's taught from the very beginning?

God wants to share life with me.

And with no complicated arguments or persuasive suggestions, He compels the walk to begin.

As I read the story of the disciples being called, I closed my eyes and imagined these men meeting Christ for the first time. They had been told by John that He was the Messiah, but they've never laid eyes on Him until now, and within a

few seconds, they have left what they were doing and are following Him.

I can't say my own conversion looked quite this seamless,
unfortunately, but the sentiment was (and is) ever-developing
within me.

What He has chosen not to reveal to me is inconsequential when compared to what He has promised me.

Journey with Me, love, and you'll see.

I love the way the Gospel of Luke describes the scene as
Jesus calls out to Simon Peter some short time after their first
encounter. Jesus climbs onto Simon Peter's boat, and after
teaching the crowds for a while, He tells Simon Peter to put
down his nets for a catch. Before he obeys the Lord, Peter
explains that they have been working all night to no avail,
but quickly finishes his thought with the words, "But at your
word I will let down the nets" (Luke 5:5).

I can't tell you for certain that I know Peter's motive for
adding the caveat, but I wonder if he wanted to make it clear
to the crowds that he was skeptical. It's amazing how quickly
we fall into patterns of self-protection when all eyes are on us,
isn't it?

Remember, Simon Peter is a man who fishes for a living. He has been working all night and has come up empty-
handed, with no reason to believe that this is going to be an
exercise that produces results. Humanly speaking, this might
be the right time to express doubt so nobody's looking his way
when it fails.

It's also significant to note that Simon Peter isn't mocking Jesus or being disrespectful to Him in his response, as evidenced by his use of the word "Master." In essence, he tells Jesus that he has tried his own plan and it didn't work.

However, Lord . . . I'm willing to give it a shot Your way.

Like you, he probably considered himself an expert in his own life and experiences, and he was stating what he believed to be a reality.

These are nets he had used many times before, and waters he had studied closely. He knew that dropping them during the day as Jesus was asking is not likely to be successful, because any good fisherman will tell you that nets are supposed to be dropped at night. It's how it's done. It's also not an easy process physically, and these men were already exhausted from being out working all night, so obedience isn't without cost.

In Simon Peter's case, the reward was swift. As the nets filled, the fisherman realized they weren't going to be able to manage the haul by themselves. They called out for others to help them. The nets that had been empty all night were now bursting, near ripping with an abundance of fish, and their boats were sinking under the weight. It was the catch of a lifetime, although Scripture doesn't give us any reason to believe they ever benefited financially from it.

Imagine the scene in your mind and allow it to become etched in your heart as you consider the way it speaks to your life now, regardless of where you are on the journey.

This is the moment for which a fisherman waits his whole life. Chaos dominates the shore as the men pull the nets in, the shouts of exertion and awe filling the air. It's a hustling, bustling mess of celebration and shock, but in the midst of it is one man who steps away from the masses.

Instead of reveling in the gift, he acknowledges the Giver.

Falling to his knees before the Lord, he utters these words: "Depart from me, for I am a sinful man, O Lord" (Luke 5:8).

The posture of his heart is bowed in reverence, not bent in obligation.

Remember? *Motivation matters.*

Jesus wasn't "shaming" Simon Peter. He didn't do this so He could embarrass him or call him a fool for suggesting it might not work.

Maybe you have seen yourself in all of your wretchedness and you can't shake free of the guilt. You wallow in your own insufficiency and can't break away from the cycle of shame in which you're caught. Instead of being empowered, you feel hopeless.

There is a difference between acknowledging our sin and allowing it to paralyze us. If you've found yourself in this particular struggle, I would urge you to take note of what happens next, because as appropriate as Simon Peter's reaction to the Lord was, it wasn't permanent.

Kneel deep with every part of yourself, yes. Confess your sin, your brokenness, your utter lack of goodness. You should feel the gravity of your own desperation, because if you don't, you'll miss the beauty of what follows.

Jesus was swift in responding to Simon Peter's request, and while He didn't correct his perspective on his own depravity, He does offer him hope.

"Do not be afraid; from now on you will be catching men" (v. 10).

In other words, *You aren't wrong about your sinfulness, but that isn't the whole story. There's work to be done for My sake and through My power, so stand up. I have plans for you.*

When I read this passage, I can't help but be struck by the symbolism.

The lowering, whether it be your net or your very body, is the right and natural response to His holiness.

And were it not for His hand upon us, we would be tempted to sink to the ocean floor where the light of day can never expose our iniquity.

But the beauty is, and has always been, in the act of rising again.

It was a net, dropped into unlikely water and brought to the surface with gasps of awe.

There is new life now—life that wasn't expected or deserved. We should marvel at the gift in the same way they did as the nets tore apart and the boats quaked with the weight of it all.

Had it not been for the overwhelming barrenness, there would not have been such appreciation for what He provided.

The true understanding of our own depravity isn't a punishment—it's an opportunity to understand the value of the gift.

So much of my time with the Lord has been spent trying to prove myself—not just to Him, but to everyone around me. I want to show myself worthy of the calling that has been placed on me, and that is where the chasing has, well, finally caught up with me.

I want to live a life that is holy because He is holy, not because I get to check it off a list. I long to have the kind of relationship with God that tells my great-grandchildren that I desired Him more than anything else offered.

I want to rely on Him wholly as I grow into what I was called to be, glorifying His name with every new bud that fights to be a flower.

After all, anyone who was there that day would have agreed that the conditions were all wrong for any good to come from fishing. They would have turned their heads, shrugged their shoulders, and called it failure.

But not Him.

It's as though He lowered Himself until He was eye-to-eye, whispering words that would change everything.

You were born for this.

I don't know why He stopped for Peter that day and I don't know why He stopped for me, but I pray I never forget the way it felt to inhale fresh air, the bitter saltwater lingering on my tongue long enough to remind me of where I had been.

What did He see? I'll never know for sure.

It was a messy, imperfect, half-filled page, yes.

But He planted the seed in barrenness, knowing full well that His love gave me no choice but to grow.

So I did what any writer would do in that situation; I turned to a new page and reached for my pencil.

Realizing, of course, I would never hold it the same way again.

CHAPTER 3

Undone

The great difficulty with many Christians is that they cannot persuade themselves that Christ (or God) loves them; and the reason why they cannot feel confident of the love of God is that they know they do not deserve his love, on the contrary, that they are in the highest degree unlovely. How can the infinitely pure God love those who are defiled with sin, who are proud, selfish, discontented, ungrateful, disobedient? This, indeed is hard to believe.

~ CHARLES HODGE

We never know when something in God's Word is going to jump out and speak in a way we weren't anticipating, and that was the case when I read Isaiah 6 a few years ago. As a bit of background info (go ahead and take five if you've memorized the entire Bible), prophets were men raised up by God in times of spiritual darkness in order to warn God's chosen people of their desperate need for repentance.

Isaiah was unusual as far as prophets were concerned as he didn't have the humble beginnings of many of the others. He wasn't a peasant or a farmer, but rather a man with royal blood who had access to many powerful men of that time period. Each prophet spoke to a specific population of people at a point in time when that group was living apart from God and his role was to prophecy about the doom that would befall them unless they changed their ways.

As you can imagine, prophets were despised by the people and ultimately most of them were martyred. With that said, when God chose each prophet, it was a done deal. They couldn't reject the call, although one of them (Jeremiah) tried to do so. Let's just say it wasn't an easy calling, but it was one that God commanded out of love for His people because He ultimately desired their return to Him as the one true God. This time period goes through a substantial amount of ebb and flow as the prophets warn the people, they shape up for a bit, and then they go back to sinning. It's a cyclical pattern that continues for approximately 500 years.

When you hear the words "minor prophet" and "major prophet," it doesn't have anything to do with characteristics of that particular person (. . . not that I ever thought it did, naturally, but you might), but rather the length of his writing included in Scripture. Because of this, Isaiah is considered a major prophet.

At the time of Isaiah's initial calling to be a prophet to Judah, King Uzziah was on the throne. For the majority of his life, King Uzziah was a good king and a man who sought after God. He was successful in battle and had the favor of the Lord until shortly before his death, when pride appears to have gotten the better of him. Despite this, he was seen as a national treasure and his death brought on a time of bitter mourning for the people.

Hopefully this little slice of background will help shape the context of what we are about to see. He's an important man who hasn't lacked for much from a human standpoint, so it's likely that he didn't realize his deep need for God until the time in his life at which we are about to look.

It appears that Isaiah entered the temple looking for consolation after the loss of the king, and it is here that we have what is one of the most dramatic interactions in the whole of Scripture.

I'm going to take a wild guess and say you haven't spent a lot of time comparing yourself to the prophets of the Old Testament. Am I right? Or maybe you have and you should have written this book instead of me.

If that's the case, I have a couple of other titles I'm happy to hand over with my full blessing and I'll stick to what I know: *fashion*.

I so wish that were true.

The part about the fashion, I mean.

You can totally still write the other books.

What I'm trying to say is that it's easy to tuck some of this away and act like it's irrelevant to our modern-day plights, but the reality is that it's shockingly applicable. No, we don't have a king and prophets, but we have the kind of hearts that can grow convinced of our lack of need for God when things seem to be going well.

It's a character trait we see represented in some way in every book of the Bible, and I believe the heart of comprehending salvation lies in understanding how imperative it is that we *need* God and not vice versa.

This is where we have to make a distinction, and it's not one I (nor should you) take lightly. Simply acknowledging that you believe something is not enough. Scripture is clear that even demons believe in the death and resurrection of Jesus (James 2:19).

So that's our topic today, friends.

Buckle up.

___

I was twenty-four years old when I became a Christian. For a good part of my days before that, He hadn't been much more than a theory I had yet to prove. And to be honest, that wasn't really a source of struggle for me.

Let's look at the facts for a minute.

By all accounts, I had a fantastic childhood. I was raised by people who loved me and believed in me, never giving me reason to feel unloved or unwanted. I didn't have a single day in my life where I worried about how I was going to get food or whether my parents could provide for me in the event of an emergency.

I didn't face sickness in any great capacity and I never experienced a major traumatic event. Was it perfect? No. But it was good enough to make me feel like God was an extra in my already-wonderful movie.

It's a blessing that I had the life I did and I certainly don't mean to paint the picture that a privileged life negates the possibility of a godly one. It isn't to disparage my parents for clothing me, caring for me, or putting me through college. Those are tremendous gifts. Yet, Scripture warns us that these things can be a stumbling block in recognizing our need for God.

That was exactly the case for me. I wasn't rebellious toward Him, I was simply unaware of my own desperation because, well, I didn't *feel* all that desperate.

Feelings are liars. We'll get to that. But go with me for right now so you'll understand the heart of what I'm saying: I just didn't have the kind of life that made me experience daily, deep, life-threatening need for Him.

I was also a pretty good kid, all things considered. I mean, I snuck out a couple (dozen-ish) times. Dad, if you read this, tell me and I'll explain everything. If I don't hear anything, I'll assume your silence means "I forgive you." Cool? I also had my fair share of alcohol-related missteps (Dad, see above statement for clarification), but on the whole I was doing all right. I hadn't gone to jail or gotten pregnant, which seemed to be the hallmark sins of people who really "needed" saving.

Sadly, it wasn't because I wasn't guilty as much as it was that I hadn't gotten *caught*.

That's a pivotal distinction, friends.

I felt like I had a hook to hang my "righteous" hat on, and I sure put a lot of stock in that piece of faulty logic.

There was also the fact I was the prototypical firstborn child, and my sister, on the other hand, made it her life's mission to be everything I wasn't.

Instead of academics, she pursued art. She wanted to make her own way in life, which was an appealing way of saying she didn't want to live in my shadow. You know, the shadow cast by the giant hat that was perilously hanging from a nonexistent hook.

I made it my business to call her out on her wrongs based on my perception of moral superiority, though. And I hope you can see how this method has a couple of features that don't lend themselves to "effective teaching."

Around middle school, she went through a Goth phase, which included a boyfriend with piercings that confused me on several levels, one of which was a basic sense of physiology that told me the ear and nose weren't designed to be connected by a chain.

I asked him about it one night at our house but he couldn't hear me on account of the fact that he was watching *The Rocky Horror Picture Show* for the hundredth time and urging us to embrace the powerful symbolism. I'm sure he had a lot to offer, but he never actually offered it. And don't think I'm making a statement about guys who wear punk shirts and dye their hair—I'm not.

And I'll go ahead and tell you that you won't like where this is eventually going if you're counting on those characteristics alone to build a case against godliness.

I had no interest in talking to him, but I was eager to make him look bad because of my frustration with Jenn. So I acted like I cared and sat down beside him.

One important thing I learned in the next ten minutes is that the smell of patchouli won't actually *kill you* after sustained contact, despite my previously held beliefs that it might.

And as you may well know, girls who own pom-poms (What? Tell me you aren't surprised I was a cheerleader . . .) are especially sensitive to it.

Still, in the interest of reaching out (*cough* self-righteousness *cough*), I persevered.

"I don't get it. Does it, like, snag on stuff? Are you afraid it'll hurt when you take it out?" Silence. His acknowledgment of the sounds coming out of my mouth hovered just below "not if my life depended on it."

I stared at Jennifer like she was a science project gone awry, rolling my eyes in disapproval. She, as you might expect, was not incredibly interested in my opinions and had very "creative" ways of reminding me of that fact. I was determined to parent her and to make her snap out of it, and she was equally convinced that she had finally found truth.

No matter what good I might have offered, it was swallowed by my intentions, never to touch the part of her that might have listened.

It went on like this for months on end.

I can still see her with her hair dyed raven-black, her hands constantly covered in paint, and her face frozen staunchly in rebellion.

I've always seen her when I looked back, but I don't believe I saw myself until recently.

On one occasion in particular, I was standing in her doorway while my parents were out, threatening her to come clean about something I thought she had done. I screamed at her and called her names, although I don't remember them now. I'm glad I don't.

She sat cross-legged on the floor with her face turned away from me, and she didn't respond, which infuriated me more. The walls were covered in obscure quotes from music I wouldn't listen to unless I was physically restrained and forced to endure as punishment.

What happened to the girl who let me curl her strawberry-kissed hair before we went to Denny's? The one that thought I hung the moon?

She had become a stranger to me, and in the darkness of her room I realized that she wanted no part of me. It cut me deep, and I retaliated.

I reached for the wrong arsenal, as we often do when we're hurt, and I inflicted wounds from the deepest part of my own insecurity.

I wanted the last word, and I got it.

She never moved.

I slammed the door and walked across the hall to my room, bright with pastel pink paint and *Teen Bop* posters. I cranked up my tape deck (worry not, wee ones, someone will explain it to you later) and flopped on my bed trying to decide what friend to call in order to process the unfortunate circumstance of being blood-related to someone so ignorant of her own failure.

She needed help, clearly.

I, on the other hand, needed a manicure before play rehearsal.

Let's just say I felt like I had the upper hand when it came to feeling like the good kid.

It's not just true for snotty ninth-graders, you know.

The assurance of an "upper hand" is indicative of one thing only, and it isn't good. It's the part of our self-awareness that whispers, "You're better off than she is." It's the lack of the one thing needed to actually move forward in knowing God.

Humility.

The basic realization that we aren't what we thought we were, necessitating a bending of the will and a reshaping of our perceived identity.

It comes in ways we don't always anticipate, and certainly in ways we might not choose.

In other words, it probably smells like patchouli.

When I read about Isaiah, I don't see a far-removed situation because God wants us to understand truth regardless of the particulars. For the first five chapters in the book of Isaiah, we hear the words of the prophet, but it's chapter 6 that brings him to a place of surrender so spectacular that it alters his entire comprehension of God.

In some sense, we all have to have a "chapter 6" experience if we are to claim we are His.

Isaiah walked into the temple that particular day because he was mourning. As you well know, the tenderness of a broken heart often allows room for new healing, and he was facing a devastating loss as well as uncertainty about what his new role would be in the wake of the king's death. He was hungry for instruction and longing for comfort, and it's safe to say that while he didn't get exactly what he came for, he got exactly what he needed.

He doesn't waste his words as he tells us what happened next:

"In the year that King Uzziah died I saw the Lord sitting upon a throne, high and lifted up; and the train of his robe filled the temple" (Isa. 6:1).

I love the confidence he has in retelling his experience. He's not concerned with what it's going to sound like to anyone else, and he isn't apologizing or explaining it away. He's stating the facts, complete with a description of the seraphim (angels) above God, one calling to another and saying, "Holy,

holy, holy is the LORD of hosts; the whole earth is full of his glory!" (v. 3).

This is the only attribute of God that is ever repeated three times in Scripture, which matters because repetition is a biblical device used to indicate the importance of the word. God's holiness is emphasized above His other characteristics, such as "loving" or "just."

Because of His holiness, it would be impossible for Isaiah to actually "see" God in His fullness, but whatever portion of God he was permitted to experience was enough to radically affect him.

The temple itself began to physically shake and fill with smoke in response to God's presence, and in the midst of it we hear the voice of Isaiah crying out as he is overcome by the realization of his own unworthiness.

"Woe is me! For I am lost; for I am a man of unclean lips, and I dwell in the midst of a people of unclean lips; for my eyes have seen the King, the LORD of hosts!" (v. 5).

As God reveals Himself, we can't help but see who we are in light of Him.

He had gone into the temple to find a respite from his sorrow and instead he came face-to-face with a reality much more traumatic than any earthly burden.

He is stricken by his own condition, and his response shows us humility at its most basic and necessary form: *I am not God. But my goodness . . . You are. Have mercy on me, Lord, I am lost.*

Some of the earliest copies of Isaiah use a word I love for "lost," indicating that Isaiah was "undone" by the presence of God. It's not a cozy moment where we get snuggled and coddled while God acquiesces to our need for approval, that's for sure.

Who would run inside to escape a storm, only to be soaked through to places we have never even felt before? To be undone by the King Himself?

As I've been describing Isaiah's experience, you've no doubt sketched it in your head, and I want to ask you an important question about your version. We touched on it earlier, but I want to circle around again as we visualize the scene.

Do you believe God was raging? Was He terrifying Isaiah, shaking His holy fists and screaming until His prophet acknowledged that he was a weak and insignificant minion? Is there a part of you that interpreted it this way? Be honest.

Is there any part of you that has interpreted Christianity this way?

If there is, I want to ask you to give this particular incident another look and allow the Lord to speak into all the other areas where you've struggled with seeing God's anger as more urgent than His love.

Isaiah didn't say he was afraid because God was frightening him.

In fact, God hadn't done a single thing outside of being present.

And that alone was enough to show the prophet who he was in light of God's tremendous love and holy mercy. This is the realization that shapes his response, and it allowed me to understand what exists underneath a majority of my misconceptions about God.

I don't believe it was God's anger that bent Isaiah's knees; it was His *love*. Can you see the difference?

We aren't forced to the ground, terror-stricken by a ruthless and cruel God.

We bow low in His presence because we see how devastatingly beautiful it is to be loved by Love Himself.

I know it to be true.

On January 17, 2001, I sat in my car while rain beat down on the windows and I considered what a dear friend had explained to me about salvation earlier that evening. I turned off my windshield wipers and my headlights and sat completely still, watching what was in front of me disappear as the rain obscured my view.

It wasn't until very recently I realized that even that was the Lord speaking to me. What a precious way to teach me, even then, that He was in the most intimate of details. Quite simply, it was much more of a surrender than it was a conversation.

Pitch-black night, rain-soaked windshield, and the sound of a song I had never heard before playing on the radio.

Looking back, I understand that when my fingers reached for the dials and buttons, I was learning the heart of discipleship. It didn't have much to do with the car, or even the day of the week or the fact that I was crying.

But it had everything to do with admitting that there's no sense in fighting over the windshield wipers with the God who created rain.

The follow-up to this realization is that if I'm afraid of driving in the rain without my wipers on, it's a little absurd to be unafraid of the One who is letting it spill.

Is it a bad thing to fear Him? No, it's actually a whole lot scarier to dismiss His majesty.

Fear and love are inextricably bound up in the true worship of God, and one without the other is, at best, man-made religion.

I listened to the words of the song playing and something in me broke. I was weak and messy and devastated as my shoulders shook in awareness of Him. I called myself a Christian before this happened, but in retrospect I don't believe I really knew what that meant.

I wholly surrendered myself to Him that night, and for the first time, I felt the gravity of what He had done for me. Not because someone told me about it or even because I read it, but because I experienced the truth of His sacrifice on such a personal level that I knew I could never deny it.

I feel things deeply and I always have; I guess I'm just carved that way. And the words I'm using here might make you think I was terrified or overwhelmed by guilt, but truly, that wasn't the case.

I was undone by His hallowed love for me, His inexplicable affection for me despite the fact that I was so incredibly undeserving of it, and the simple and indisputable way I finally rested in awe of who He was.

I didn't repeat specific phrases, but the posture of my heart toward God changed. To be totally honest, I don't remember much of what I physically said or didn't say, but I have no question that this was the point at which I stepped from death to life.

As I sit and write these words, I have on my desk a receipt from my car that night. On the back of it, I had scribbled all the lyrics I could remember from the song that was playing (it wasn't a Christian station, by the way) because I didn't want to forget them.

It's wrinkled and weathered now, but the words are still as clear on paper as they are in my heart. They're etched into me, undeniable in their poetic assurance of what I have found to be true since then. I love these words from the song:

> *Completely incomplete*
> *I'll take your invitation*
> *You take all of me now . . .*

He is a God who deserves the glory we offer in our meagerness, and He can be trusted with our lives. He is good, and He is a promise-keeper. He is all the things He claims to be and He delights in us as His children. He is our Father, our safe-haven, and our comfort.

But more than that, He is *holy.*

He isn't defined by where we position Him in our lineup of priorities; He is fully defined by Himself.

I would have told you I believed in Him before that night, but I had never felt my need for Him. Head knowledge, not heartbreak over sin. I had never experienced repentance.

I know.

That word can bring so many images, and for me, none of them were as tied to a holy God as they were a man on a street corner, frenetically shouting "REPENT!" in a way that looked more like a drug overdose than a biblical mandate.

When you hear the word "repent," is it the voice of a madman or the command of a loving God?

Unfortunately, we've likely confused the two, and it's costing us dearly.

This part of the book is really hard for me to write, because I am one of many who were influenced by "Christians" who didn't portray the difference very well.

They made me feel more judged than loved and it scrambled up the pieces for me. It was me against them and God was on their side.

We are saints and you are a sinner. *Repent.*

We're going to heaven and you're going to hell. *Repent.*

God loves us and hates you. *Repent.*

Whether or not they used those words was irrelevant; the message was clear:

It's us against you and God is on our side.

Here's the truth of the matter:

God is on God's side.

We are born in a state that puts us at odds with Him.

The reconciliation that takes place came at a great cost to Him and puts the burden of glory-giving on us.

If you've been healed by God, it wasn't so you could ridicule the sick.

It's so you could tell them what the Healer did for you.

Come and sit with me for a minute while the rain pours, will you? Because I want you to see what led to grieving my own sin that night. I want you to know why I fear Him, reverence Him, and find absolute joy in bowing down before Him. Do you want to know what brought the bitter sting of sorrow while I cried out?

The sheer madness of His love for me.

Genuine repentance doesn't happen when people put us in a corner; it happens when we realize God chose us in spite of the fact that we would never have chosen Him.

Oftentimes people would rather force-feed guilt to those they disagree with than swallow the grace that declares them equally unworthy.

I should know.

Because I was all too happy to stand in a doorway instead of walking into my sister's room.

It's the reason she never turned around.

It wasn't my love that asked her to listen; it was my arrogance. And she knew the difference.

We all do.

The satisfaction that comes from slamming doors reveals how little we know of His love and how easily we mistake loudness for righteousness. It makes us look like fools, not saints.

God came to us wrapped in flesh, choosing humility from the stable to the cross, and it is humility that ushers us into His holiness and beckons us to follow the well-worn path traveled by the saints before us.

I knew I was loved. And one rainy night in Nashville I understood why that mattered so much.

> Then one of the seraphim flew to me,
> having in his hand a burning coal that he
> had taken with tongs from the altar. And he
> touched my mouth and said: "Behold, this
> has touched your lips; your guilt is taken
> away, and your sin atoned for." (Isa. 6:6–7)

Isaiah was healed, his guilt removed from him forevermore. Nothing he could do, say, feel, or think from that moment could change the fact that he belonged to God. No catch. No requirements. He was irreversibly, irrevocably, and wholly made right with God.

Up until this moment, God hasn't even spoken to Isaiah. He has simply been *there*. He has allowed him to glimpse His holiness, and no words are necessary for revelation of such majesty. But now . . .

"And I heard the voice of the Lord saying, 'Whom shall I send, and who will go for us?'"

He speaks. *God Himself speaks.*

His voice echoes throughout the temple, and Isaiah is so in awe of the Lord that he can barely wait for the question to be posed before he answers emphatically, "Here I am! Send me" (v. 8).

Understand what is happening here: Isaiah is offering his full, unquestioning service to the Lord. He isn't begrudgingly going along with it, and he certainly isn't expressing any fear as to what the next steps will look like. His motivation is pure and immediate, born of a deep desire to be used by the One who healed him.

Let us look upon our journey with God in the same manner. We will never make much progress if our motivation is anything less than gratitude in motion, rooted in the deep and abiding love of the One who loved us first.

God has given us each a unique charge—a calling in life that will involve aspects we don't enjoy. In Isaiah's case, he knew this meant he was going to be a man who was frequently dismissed, and likely worse. But it pales in comparison to the mercy that has captured him, and instead of being fearful, he is eager to begin his journey.

John Calvin gives a beautiful exposition of Isaiah's response:

> *Here am I.* So ready a reply shows how great is that cheerfulness which springs from faith; for he who but lately lay like a dead man dreads no difficulty. Hence we see that the amazement of which we have formerly

spoken did not spring from rebellion, in wishing to flee from God, or to refuse the charge which had been laid upon him; but because he needed new grace, that he might know that he would be able to endure the burden. On this account it ought to be observed, that we cannot undertake anything in a proper manner without the evidence of our calling; otherwise we shall pause and hesitate at every step.

Besides, it is a powerful aid to our confidence, when we know that we are not destitute of the necessary gifts, but that God has bestowed them on us, in order that we may be better enabled to discharge our office. Now, this remarkable instance of obedience ought to produce such an effect on our minds that we shall readily and cheerfully undertake any task which he may be pleased to enjoin, and shall never refuse any task, however difficult we may imagine it to be. *When the Prophet says, Here am I, the meaning is, that he is ready to obey the commands of God; for this mode of expression is frequently employed in Scripture to denote obedience.* (emphasis added)[4]

Three words uttered in response to our awareness of a holy
God who has accepted us, made us righteous, and rescued us
from the clutches of death. With full knowledge that what is
up ahead will likely be difficult, we cannot help but join in
Isaiah's hearty acceptance of God's will for our lives.

Immediately the Lord gave Isaiah his mission: "Go, and
say to this people . . ." (v. 9).

He didn't paint an optimistic picture of how they would
respond to the call to repentance, either. He essentially told
Isaiah that they weren't going to listen to him, and that they
were going to continue to ignore God.

At one point Isaiah asked the Lord how long this will go
on, and again, the answer wasn't what he hoped. While God
didn't give him a specific number of years, He indicated that
it would continue until the land was desolate and the cities
were uninhabited (v. 11).

God's people were going to remain rebellious for quite
some time, but Isaiah's call didn't change in response to that
fact. In some sense you may be like me, wondering why God
would call a prophet to speak to a nation that will ignore him
and the God he serves. It feels a little bit like a waste of time,
and maybe even a cruel trick.

And this is where we need to pause. Pull back the lens.
Remember what we know about the character of God and
process what we are reading in light of that.

God was giving Isaiah a call to obedience.

In addition, and because of His love for him, He fore-
warned Isaiah that his efforts were going to appear fruitless.

He wasn't setting him up to fail. He knew what His people were going to choose because He is omniscient, and He allowed Isaiah to see a little bit behind the scenes.

Here's the part where we need to listen in, because He's speaking to us as well.

"You met Me here, and you knew I was the God I claimed I was. You confessed your need for Me and your desire to serve Me, and I commanded you to go. Whether or not they repent is not your concern, nor is the number of days I will use your mouth as Mine. You have offered yourself to Me, and as a willing servant, you have only one duty in the matter: Go. Leave the rest to Me."

Our call is to obey Him, but that doesn't mean we won't ever doubt or ask Him to clarify our task; we say it in a thousand different ways, but the question remains the same: *How long, O Lord?*

It isn't about a nation of stiff-necked people, but the sentiment hasn't changed; *I will journey with You, yes. But what will this look like a little farther down the road?*

We don't get the privilege of knowing the answer as clearly as Isaiah did, but I hope you see the bigger issue.

Even if we did, it wouldn't change a thing.

Even if He allowed us to see the darkest nights ahead or the ecstatic joy that awaited us, it would not change the call that was issued on our lives to obey Him.

We are given the same information Isaiah was and we are asked to respond in the same manner.

For all practical purposes, the windshield view is irrelevant. You can chase it if you like, but it will only lead you back to the quaking temple, demanding you to trust His ways above your own.

God assured Isaiah that although he wouldn't see a revival of the people, a "holy seed" would remain. The land will be ravaged and it will look hopeless for a while, but there is a remnant that will follow the true gospel (v. 13).

This seed represents those who have been set apart by His grace, and no drought or famine can prevent it from growing in likeness to Him.

We have been "born again, not of perishable seed but of imperishable, through the living and abiding word of God" (1 Pet. 1:23).

A seed He saw as worth growing.

Here we see Christ; the wonderful, holy, life-giving Love made flesh for our sake, and we see with new eyes the cost of what He has planted.

A blood-soaked crown of thorns piercing Him as they ridiculed His claims of sovereignty.

The weight of sin in its entirety pressed into Him while they cast lots to see who would claim His clothing. And in the midst of it all, laboring for breath, He uttered these words.

"They know not what they do . . ."

No, they didn't. They couldn't have.

Because suspended on a cross before them was the One who pleaded mercy on our behalf as we spit on Him in our disbelief.

We stand in the shadow of a cross on Calvary, and though we look there no more to find Him, we should take care to never forget what held Him there.

Love.

His wounds have healed you; His cross lowered in death to raise you to life.

I have seen enough of Him to believe it is so, and my mouth calls out before my mind dares to object:

Here am I, the beloved of Christ . . .

Send me, Lord, for I know no other way to love You in return.

CHAPTER 4

An Affair of the Will

But the great thing to remember is that, though our feelings come and go,
His love for us does not. It is not wearied by our sins, or our indifference;
and therefore, it is quite relentless in its determination that we shall be
cured of those sins, at whatever cost to us, at whatever cost to Him.

~ C. S. LEWIS

I n the second letter Paul wrote to the Corinthian church,
we can hear the impassioned commission he issued: *You*
believe what I have told you concerning the Christ, and you have
made strides. But do not let yourselves fall away from what you
know to be truth.

He acknowledges the trials that they will come up against,
and he also tells them that he himself has faced difficulties in
his faith. Essentially, the letter is written to encourage them to
continue living lives that glorify God despite the way it looks
or feels.

It's advice we can't afford to proceed without hearing, because the truth of the matter is this: *There is hardly a worse way to approach your faith than by allowing your emotions to dictate your course.*

I can't tell you how many times I've doubted God's presence in my life because I didn't "feel" like He was near me. And countless nights I have offered prayers to a God I could no more sense than I could play a game of hopscotch with. It seemed to me that I was having a one-way conversation based on my own creation, and it genuinely made me question whether or not anyone was (or had ever been) listening.

Christ Himself warned us that we were going to be up against opposition, but maybe you have tucked those words away in an "optional" folder. If that's the case, when you do hit a rough patch, you're going to wonder why. You're going to ask what you've done wrong, or maybe why He doesn't care about you. You're going to do all the things that rational people do in rational situations, and you're going to narrow down the list of possibilities into something that looks vaguely like this:

1. He doesn't really exist.
2. If He does, He doesn't seem to love me.
3. Maybe I've done something wrong.
4. I need to make up for it and get back on sure footing with Him.

We test the waters of faith with instruments He has warned us against using, and then we try and make sense of the lie we are calling truth.

Clearly, this is a fool-proof plan.

I know, I know. But seeing that on paper doesn't make it go away in experience. We want to do whatever it is we are supposed to be doing as followers of Christ, but unfortunately if our theology doesn't match our daily approach to struggle we aren't going to get very far.

Over and over again in Paul's letter, he urges his listeners to look past their current conditions and seek ways to bring glory to God in spite of the situation, and that doesn't happen by waiting to feel differently about it. And here's where we get into a verse I happen to love, love, love. It's jam-packed with goodness and practical application.

Paul says, "For Christ's love compels us, since we have reached this conclusion: If One died for all, then all died. And He died for all so that those who live should no longer live for themselves, but for the One who died for them and was raised" (2 Cor. 5:14–15 HCSB).

Ahhhh. This one's got some power. Let's dig in before we take our next steps with Him.

He starts out by telling them what the impetus behind their seeking a godly life should be—and it isn't "because it feels good and comfy." In fact, it's hardly even a call to action. It's a blatant statement about what the driving force is in our pursuing of holiness, and surprise, surprise . . . it's not something we do.

Christ's love compels us.

In other words, we cannot help but to desire to be more like Him. Once we understand the love He has poured out, we are bound to follow through with action.

And the process of becoming more like Him is called sanctification; put simply, it's just the way we move toward righteousness and away from sin in our lives. We won't (in this life) ever be fully sanctified because we live in bodies that aren't capable of perfection, but because of His love, we push ourselves to grow more like Him every day.

The word *compels* in Greek is *synechō,* and among its meanings are words we might expect, such as "urge" and "impel." One of the descriptions I love is this: "To hold together; to press on every side; to hold completely."[5]

It isn't even that we are "led" to do something godly; it's that we are essentially pressed into the mold that shapes us, and we are held together there. It's more than a feeling of "wanting to do something"; it's a new comprehension of the fact that He has chosen to give us the option and now makes it virtually impossible for us to go on as true believers without regard to His best for us.

One of the definitions even goes so far as to say it is likened to a farm animal being pushed on every side so it can't move.

If that doesn't sound applicable or loving yet (and indeed I agree that it doesn't), let me finish.

In this example, it is because the farmer needs to administer medication, and therefore, creates a situation where the animal will be still *so it can be healed*.

Let me ask you a logical follow-up here: Do you think the animal is excited about what he perceives is happening? Does it seem like it's a fun moment? Doubtful.

But the farmer knows better, and therefore, he presses past the emotional response in order to do what needs to be done. Because he knows what we need even when we don't.

A few verses before this Scripture Paul reminds us that our "light momentary affliction is preparing us for an eternal weight of glory beyond all comparison, as we look not to the things seen but to the things that are unseen. For the things that are seen are transient, but the things that are unseen are eternal" (2 Cor. 4:17–18).

He is reminding us that all these things that seem to be out of place, inconvenient, or even downright horrifying to us in our earthly understanding are simply not of consequence in light of what is coming.

But guess what?

He doesn't tell us we have to *feel* that way. In the very next verse, Paul says, "because we have concluded this: that one has died for all." Not, "we think Jesus died" or "it seems reasonable to say it's likely" or even "we are so convinced by our own experience" or "we feel that . . ."

We have concluded.

We have decided to believe, despite any evidence to the contrary, and we will continue to live our lives in obedience as a response to that fact. We have taken Him at His Word, we have offered ourselves to Him, and in order for the seed to grow and produce the finest fruit, we must rely on the Holy Spirit to enable us to obey His commands.

Allow this to be a reminder to you in the moments where you feel unsure about whether or not God loves you, or when you doubt what His intentions are for your life. We carry an impossible burden unless we set our minds like flint, determined at every pass to elevate His Word above our own perceptions.

At first, this sounded harsh to me. It looked a little like He was basically saying, "It isn't going to look good, feel good, or ever really be what you're trying to make it. And that's your problem, not Mine."

I genuinely believed that I just had to get to a place where I could break through my own doubts and feel completely secure, and in those attempts, I failed.

God-chaser, party of one.

The more we tell ourselves we can make it feel perfect, the less we realize that His promises and His character are based on a foundation far more steady than any momentary euphoric experience we can have. And when we stop looking for those things to give us peace, we can begin to abide instead of frantically seek what we believe is the goal.

From a practical standpoint, how do we do that?

I must defer to the great words of C. S. Lewis on the matter, because I certainly can't come close to capturing the heart of following Christ in a more profoundly applicable statement.

"People are often worried . . . they are told they ought to love God. They cannot find any such feelings in themselves. What are they to do? The answer is the same as before. *Act as if you did*. Do not sit trying to manufacture feelings. Ask yourself, 'If I were sure that I loved God, what would I do?' When you have found the answer, *go and do it*" (emphasis added).[6]

You might not ever be fully, unquestionably, unswervingly convinced that God loves you, or that you love Him in return for that matter. It's not because it's not true, but because you're a finite human being trying to understand something that you weren't created to thoroughly comprehend. Often times, the best thing we can do is continue saying we believe Him in spite of the fact that we don't have the emotional counterpart in the measure we wish we did.

And God isn't punishing you if you don't feel it. In fact, He's telling you something you might never have fully considered until now: *It's not required*.

Sit there, just for a moment.

Think of the times when a friend was telling you about how confident she was, how utterly moved she had been by an encounter with the Lord. You wrestled inwardly, wondering if you had even met the God she was referring to, and if you had, why He wasn't allowing you the same experience. It makes us feel like we're missing something or that we aren't where we're supposed to be spiritually, when really, following Christ isn't based on what we can see of Him. It's believing He has shown us enough of Himself to trust Him with what we can't see.

And the most beautiful, sacrificial, God-glorifying moments don't necessarily come when we feel fully convinced. I believe the times when I stand, face to the wind, telling Him I am choosing to trust Him even though I can't emotionally sense His presence are the instances He rejoices over my faith the most.

I love that Isaiah had a moment where he knew beyond a shadow of a doubt that he was in the presence of the Lord, but I don't think our response must be determined by that same assurance.

More often than not, we aren't going to have that radical revelation, and yet it is our will that continues to bow before Him with the words that rattle hell with their faith.

I don't see You, but I am believing that You see me.

As Christians, we don't always have a strong sense of His voice or presence as far as tangible, earth-shattering evidence, but we do have the gift of the Holy Spirit within us. We might not "hear" God, but we learn to trust the promptings we are given by His Spirit, and we act in accordance with that urging. God isn't making it a game where some people wander around wondering what they're supposed to be doing and others have a navigation-like voice directing their every step.

The mistake we make is in assuming our feelings indicate the quality of our faith.

As a result, some people "are waiting to have an inward feeling that His words are true, before they will believe them. They look upon them as beautiful things for Him to say, and they wish they could believe them, but they do not think they can be true in their own special case, unless they have an inward feeling that they are; and if they should speak out honestly, they would confess that, since they have no such inward feeling, they do not believe His words apply to them; and as a consequence they do not in the least expect Him to actually care for their affairs at all. 'Oh, if I could only feel it was all true,' we say; and God says, 'Oh, if you would only believe it is all true!'"[7]

When we spend more of our time searching for assurance than we do acting out of belief, we are chasing God.

This came as a startling realization to me, because I am an emotional, experiential, and very intuitive person. So when I couldn't have that with the Lord, I saw myself as a failure, or worse yet, someone who hadn't tried hard enough to achieve it.

Maybe you want to shout along with Moses, "Show me Your glory!"

But allow yourself to ask which two words are more important, and your answer will reveal your true devotion.

I chased God, shouting, *"Show me."*

Truly abiding in Christ means whispering in every instance, "Your glory. Only Your glory, Lord."

We may see His glory and we may not, but we do well to remember that His glory remains regardless. We will have moments where we experience a sense of Him that is overwhelming and poetic, where the curtain is pulled back a bit on His essence. But those moments shouldn't dictate our behavior, nor should we faultily assume they are the result of it.

I believe that one of the ways the enemy convinces us that we aren't "good Christians" is by tempting us to believe we don't know Him because we don't sense Him all the time. If you're more reliant on the feeling than you are obedience, you're going to chase Him forever.

This journey with our Lord is about conforming to Him, and in our sanctification, our lives will show evidence of our spiritual maturity. We will take on more and more characteristics of our God, and our attitudes and behavior will be different. But don't think it's something you're in control of, or that it's a project God dumped in your lap and told you to complete.

Paul explains, "And we all, with unveiled face, beholding the glory of the Lord, are being transformed into the same image from one degree of glory to another. For this comes from the Lord who is the Spirit" (2 Cor. 3:18).

We need to remember that the phrase "being transformed" is in a passive tense, indicating that we aren't in charge of transforming ourselves; it's the work of the Holy Spirit within us. We willingly allow it, though, and we can certainly thwart it. So it's not to say we don't play a role, but we aren't (and can't be) the one who does the transforming.

So the sermon notes, the stacks of Christian books, and all the fellowship potlucks you have on your calendar are a waste of time if you aren't relying on Him. Our strength is simply not enough to make us grow in holiness.

It's another reason to step back a bit and reassess our duties as believers, ensuring that we haven't loaded on

responsibilities and obligations that He has not issued to us.
Our role is so simple that most believers fight it:

*Obey what I have revealed to you, no matter the cost, and in
so doing you will grow more like me.*

That's the call of discipleship, regardless of how much
more complicated your mind wants to make it. We show our
love to the Lord by obeying Him. Plain and simple. It certainly isn't an easy process, but it's the pruning and replanting
of aspects that aren't in alignment to His that bring life where
death once was.

> We offer the discipline, and "that dis-
> cipline becomes a means of grace through
> which God works and moves to transform
> that dead portion of our body into life in the
> image of Christ. One day you wake up and
> discover, often to your amazement, that the
> discipline is no longer a discipline; it is now
> the natural outflow of a being that has been
> raised to new life in Christ—that the Spirit
> of the One who raised Christ Jesus from the
> dead, the Spirit who also dwells in you, has
> made alive your dead body also. You did not
> do it. God did it. But God did it through the
> discipline you offered."[8]

I will tell you from my own personal experience that the
times I am walking the closest to Him (through prayer, Bible
study, worship, etc. . . .) are when I am most likely to feel that

I can rest in His promises. It's no surprise that this is the case, but oftentimes I think we underestimate the power of obedience where we might be more likely to strive for answers.

I cannot count the number of times I have been at the end of my rope about something going on in my life. I would spend days (months? years?) trying to figure out how I could change a characteristic about myself that I knew wasn't godly. And no matter how many approaches I took, it was (at best) a temporary and surface level bandage that would rip open at the first sign of struggle.

I had convinced myself that I just wasn't going to become a godly woman like all the other godly women around me.

I would watch others and I couldn't help but compare myself, always landing on the same frustration; *I can't make myself look like them.* When I read passages like the one above, I feel a peace that reminds me that He never asked me to.

And what gives me the most hope is the simple fact that eluded me for such a long time.

He isn't saying He will try to *help*.

He's promising He will *transform us*.

It is a process. We will have to give up our own agenda and trust in His, over and over again. We can't see the end result, but He can, and He is everyday urging us one step closer to it.

In the dark of night, 2,000 years ago, Jesus left a linen shroud and an empty grave, along with the imprints of His feet in the words of Scripture.

Whether or not you feel like it's true is irrelevant.

I can't help but hear the echo of a man, begging for healing as he came across Jesus one day, saying, "I believe; help my unbelief!" (Mark 9:24).

It isn't a contradiction; it is a confirmation of our humanity due to our sin nature, despite the desire to believe perfectly. With our mouths we say "I believe," and with our hearts we confess our inability to eliminate doubt. Our actions should always come from what we know is true, not what we are struggling to fully embrace in that truth.

Jesus knows the deepest measure of our own motivation. He fully recognizes the difference in a person who doubts while he earnestly seeks God and a person who rejects God entirely. Instead of rebuking the man, He honors the plea for faith and heals his son.

It's interesting to note that the man had gone to the disciples (presumably believing they could heal his son) before he went to Christ, but they were not able to cast out the demon. It stands to reason that his belief in Christ's ability may have wavered because of the disciples' failure, and by the time he spoke to Jesus, the word "if" had worked its way into his vocabulary. We are reminded that even today, the perceived inability of others has no relevance to the ability of God, nor can it change the sovereign will of God.

I love this story and the heart of the man who came to Jesus out of desperation, hungry to fill the gaps in his faith with belief. And what is the first thing he does in order to make progress in that direction?

He says he believes.

Do you think he *felt* differently after he stated it? Probably not. Let's remember the scene at this point: his son is writhing on the ground in agony and he has no reason to believe that's going to change based on physical evidence.

I often read a story in Scripture and imagine that the person in the account has a realization of what eventually happens. I miss the fact that they can only see what I can in my life: exactly what is before me at that very moment.

He doesn't know that his son is about to be healed.

But he says he believes.

And many, many times in our lives as Christians, we will be standing in the midst of what looks to us to be chaos, not knowing what the next scene will bring.

That is the place of true faith. It's the space between, where we declare it without having seen the miracle yet.

I'm willing to bet that after the man watched his son be completely healed and restored to life, his feelings about belief changed. And many people today live out their faith the same way, telling the Lord they will believe when they see proof of Him.

We chase Him, don't we?

Don't wait for the miracle you think will make it clear. Confess your belief and then act out of that determination.

> Nobody can always have devout feel-
> ings: and even if we could, feelings are not
> what God principally cares about. Christian
> love, either towards God or towards man,

is an affair of the will. If we are trying to do His will we are obeying the commandment, "Thou shalt love the Lord thy God." He will give us feelings of love if He pleases. We cannot create them for ourselves, and we must not demand them as a right. But the great thing to remember is that, though our feelings come and go, His love for us does not. It is not wearied by our sins, or our indifference; and, therefore, it is quite relentless in its determination that we shall be cured of those sins, at whatever cost to us, at whatever cost to Him.[9]

We don't follow Him because we are moved to do so or because we think we're sufficiently prepared. We don't wait for a moment of emotional revelation. We simply fix our eyes, steady ourselves with His promises, and put one foot resolutely in front of the other out of obedience.

And when the feelings of unbelief come like clouds on the path, we form these words alone with our lips, and we step forward anyway.

Lord . . . *I believe.*

CHAPTER 5

Platitudes and Lace

But I cannot, by direct moral effort, give myself new motives. After the first few steps in the Christian life we realize that everything which really needs to be done in our souls can be done only by God.

~ C. S. Lewis

———————

F rom the moment the girls told me we were going to "pray over our house," I was panicked. What does that even mean? Do you talk out loud? Are you supposed to intertwine your fingers, clasp them together, or hold someone else's when you "pray over" something?

Is it weird? Because it sounds weird.

There are a lot of hurdles to becoming a Christian as an adult and not having any idea what you're supposed to do with your hands.

I've been in a hundred million social circles in my life, but Christianity proved to be the hardest cultural adjustment. It wasn't because people weren't kind and patient with me. I just didn't know the lingo. I didn't know the drill. I was trying to blend in, but even the word *believer* sort of sounded like a creepy pretense for beginning a relationship.

I considered getting one of those fish stickers for my back window, because I felt like it said, "It's cool, I'm one of you" in a powerful way to all the drivers I was trying to get in front of in traffic. And naturally, I would need a cross necklace. That's a given. Charm bracelet with the symbols from Revelation? Bonus points.

I could fake all that, no problem. But praying out loud? Yeah, they're going to know this thing fits me like a pair of size 12 shoes.

Not to mention, it sounded weird. I may have alluded to this.

I was in class the day we were going to have the ritual-deal, so I kept thinking about it. I got more and more nervous as the hours ticked by. This was going to be a train wreck. Honestly, it was terrifying.

Five o'clock came and I started to pack up my books. I said a quick prayer that went something like this:

> "Hey God. I know I'm new here. I'm
> really hoping to not screw this up. Can You
> give me a hand?"

I had preprogrammed a Christian radio station into my car in case the others (read, "THE BELIEVERS") were traveling with me. I didn't dig the music and it mostly all sounded the same to me, but if there was a rule book, surely that was in there. Which almost made up for the lack of a sketched-fish sticker, yes?

I went ahead and listened in case God wanted to talk to me through the deejay. Or maybe He could say something in a song? What if I hit the jackpot and they had to PRAY for a listener; and then maybe I could clue in to the key words? Totally worth a shot. They went through two songs about how Jesus died for us and that He loves us. I was about to change it because this is stuff I already knew.

The guy deejay came back on right before I clicked away and he and the lady started chatting about something. Honestly, I don't have the slightest clue what they talked about, but at one point I remember her saying, "Yes. But when you know that you are hidden in the shadow of His wings, you feel safe."

Hey roomies? Mama's got a new catchphrase.

I pulled into the driveway, ace in my prayer-pocket, and decided I might survive this moment after all. All the girl's cars were there when I pulled up, so I knew it was go-time. I walked in the house, set down my backpack, and waited for further instruction.

I could hear voices from the back of the house.

"Hey Ang! We're just getting started! We're in the back bedroom." I started walking in that direction. So the calm lasted all of fifteen seconds and now I was back to thinking this was going to be the end of my Christian friend career.

As soon as I turned the corner I could see them all huddled in a circle. Okay . . . circle. Got it. We form a circle when we pray over things. Check.

Were they hand-holding? No. No they were not. Good to know.

I walked in and they made a little gap for me.

"Hi," I whispered. And then I prayed to become invisible, which apparently God wasn't honoring because they were all staring at me like my face was on fire.

Or maybe they weren't. Maybe that's just the look people get when they're about to start this sort of event. I decided maybe I shouldn't be smiling in that case because this was going to be holy, so I thought about something sad and braced myself for step two.

Jen started.

"Okay, y'all. Let's hold hands and pray over Julie's room, okay?"

Hands! I did not see that coming. But I acted like I did.

Now what? Eyes open? Heads bowed? Is there going to be singing? Because I don't know any Christian songs. I really, really hope there is no singing.

I didn't have time to think. The heads went down and the eyes closed. Hands. Heads. Eyes. Check, check, check.

My life goal at this point in time was not all that dissimilar from the rest of my early Christian days. Blend in. That's it. Just try to bleeeeend in.

Jen prayed something really pretty, and I realized that the girls to my right and left were probably aware of my sweaty hands by the time she got to "Amen."

It seemed like a bad first date, this "praying out loud" thing. You don't feel like you know what you're saying or doing and there's no sense pretending you didn't just wipe your hands all the way down your jeans to dry them off. I smiled at the girls, bobbing my head in recognition of the first phase being complete.

We moved to the next room. The family room.

"Ang, will you cover this one for us?" Jen asked.

"I would love to."

Or I would rather welcome toothpicks in my retinas. Either way.

We held hands again and everyone put their heads down. I did the same. And then I started.

I don't remember the exact words, but it went something like this:

"Jesus, thank You for this house and for these friends. I'm asking that You give us a lot of wonderful times here in this family room. I'm so happy we will have cable, and that we have couches."

Couches? Really? Surely God was cringing on my behalf. I mean, are you even supposed to say "cable" in a prayer? Can I GET A PLAYBOOK HERE?

It was going downhill fast, but I resisted panic, knowing full well that the closer was going to seal the deal. *Get to your money-maker, Ang . . . time's a wastin' . . .*

"And also that You will just keep us hiding in the shadow of Your wings. Amen." There was *mmm*-ing, which I had ascertained from the previous prayer was a sign of "prayer-acceptance."

"Angie, I love it when you pray out loud. It's so soothing," Jen said. And there wasn't a hint of sarcasm. They were all so genuinely supportive of me trying to get it right and they accepted me exactly where I was with the kind of love that makes it hard to resist. I still smile when I think about it. Mostly because of how kind they were, but also because I really did say "couches."

We moved on to the other rooms and eventually my hands stopped shaking and sweating. We even prayed over the bathroom. That was really interesting. We all giggled and I was pleasantly surprised to see that laughing and praying out loud could happen together.

I hadn't seen that coming either.

So this new house, much like my faith, didn't have any furniture yet. But it was set up with love and ready to be made into a home. I will never forget that moment, or the complete unawareness I had of the entire purpose of the "prayer meeting."

While I was praying to impress them, they were praying to be impressed by Him.

Looking back, I know that God didn't cringe because I said the word "cable," nor did He rebuke me for not understanding. But He did put me in the middle of a family room with a group of girls that would teach me the difference between talking to your friends with your eyes closed and realizing that you can actually approach the throne of God with your words.

It wasn't until much later that I learned that the phrase "shadow of your wings" is actually in the Bible. Like, you know, other people have read it and it wasn't just me and the deejay. I chuckled when I found out because I remembered how proud I was to have something that made it look like I knew what I was doing.

Note to self: *Nobody knows exactly what they're doing, and the ones that copy other people are the least likely to admit it.*

I recall a conversation between me and the Lord that happened a few nights after the infamous "praying over the family room" incident.

I thanked Him for helping me not die of embarrassment or fear. I also mentioned the invisibility thing would have been an awesome touch. As I recall, He didn't address that in His response, but He taught me something in that moment that I have never forgotten. It wasn't His voice, but it was Him speaking, and I knew it instantly.

THIS is what I want.

I laid very still in my bed and considered that what He was saying was that all the pretty words in the world didn't compare to coming to Him with an open heart. I can converse with the God who threw the stars in their places and rest in knowing that He wants that more than perfect phrasing.

With that said, I will always err on the side of full disclosure in this book, and the truth is I still get a little nervous to pray out loud. That's silly, I guess, but it's true. And as much as I try and stay away from all of the "wing-shadow" prayers, they do slip out occasionally. And He always reminds me that when I do that, I'm not really talking to Him.

I'm talking to them and I'm assuming He's listening.

It's human nature and I don't think it's the end of the world to just call a spade a spade and recognize that we are going to have to deal with this kind of thing, but it's also important that we really believe we have the ear of God.

When I am walking around the pool and I see a woman who looks like a vision in her bathing suit, I get a little critical of myself. Which is a nice way of saying, "Maybe You could relocate her to another nice little neighborhood and she can take all of her perfect children with her. Amen."

Again, real life breeds real thoughts, right?

And certainly at that point I could say to the Lord, "Oh, mighty Jesus, King of all things good and holy and magnificent . . . I shall not allow my thoughts of jealousy to persevere . . . *Whaaaaat?!?!?!*"

Listen. He knows that the response to her in my heart was not that, umm, fancy-looking.

And there's a part of me that thinks it means more to Him to just say that instead of dressing it up. After I give Him the gut-honest response, I say something like this:

"I'm a mess, God. I know You don't see me the way I do. Please help me get a better handle on my self-loathing. And also, please hide the chips. Amen."

I don't need the platitudes and lace. I need Him.

This has really changed the way I pray; not just when I'm in front of other people, but even in my private dialogue with the Lord. It eliminated the image I have unintentionally carried with me for the last decade, and maybe it's one you've had as well.

Prayer time must look like this:

> The room is clean and a gentle breeze
> is flowing in from the half-open ("ajar" if
> you are speaking directly to God) window.
> You have the Bible as well as several books
> open to well-marked pages. The sent of lilac
> drifts from a candle while you consider the
> meaning of multisyllable (and preferably not
> English) words. You have naturally settled
> into your prayer rug before you begin, and
> the stillness of the room calls you to a place
> of ecstatic worship, where you feel wholly,
> completely connected to the Lord.

Well, that sounds fantastic.

But there are Cheerios ground up into the carpet and it smells like a wet dog.

So there's that.

But guess what? He wants to be with me here.

He wants to be with you there.

I'll never wrap my brain around that idea, but am I so grateful for it. I can talk to Him about my not-so-pretty life and I don't have to wait for the perfect moment. In fact, that's not the goal.

Am I saying that there's something wrong with having an area where you go pray? Absolutely not! That's wonderful. But don't for a second believe that God wants your prayers to be only those locked behind those doors.

He doesn't want the right words or setting; He wants the ripe heart.

I hear people talk about how silly it is to pray to God for a parking spot. Okay, so maybe that isn't the biggest life-crisis we face, but why not? Now, if that's the only thing you say to Him all day, you might want to reconsider, but if it's just a part of your conversation with Him, then so be it.

I can walk around my house and say things like this, "Oh, Lord. I don't know what to say to her. She is making me crazy and I don't want to make a mess of the whole relationship, but it isn't right. What do I say? I really need Your help, God. Give me wisdom."

And then a few minutes later, "Help me find peace in this mess of a house. I'm so tired."

And I thank Him all the time for small things as well as big. "Thank You for the rain, Lord." "I love this house." "Oh, my kids are playing kindly. I'm so grateful for that."

Sometimes, just this: "Be with me, Lord."

Over and over and over, because the other words are hidden in there too. I don't need to wrap letters around them because He doesn't need them to understand my heart.

It's not often that easy in real life, though. Not even for those who walked right alongside Him. We can't help but feel like there has to be a "system" for prayer that maybe we aren't quite getting right, so we search for it instead of just obeying what He has commanded. In other words, we spend more time talking about how wonderful it is to hide under His wings than actually finding refuge there.

━━━━━━━━━━

Like any person who makes a habit of chasing God, all the things I struggle with eventually boil down to the disenchanting realization that I am not, in fact, the center of the universe.

And I do not, contrary to my frequent presumptions, affect every situation from potty-training to global warming.

It's a wake-up call, I can tell you that.

All this time we spend trying to create the perfect prayer life is, in effect, an extreme case of "missing the point."

And not even just for the obvious reasons, either. Once I really studied what the Lord asks of us as far as prayer, I was totally convicted about the way I had been approaching it.

So let's start with the basics. Why do we pray?

Because God commands us to.

Next?

We become so good at giving Christian answers that we start to look like the kid in class who raises her hand and wiggles in her chair desperately until she's called on so she can announce the correct (and obvious . . . *duh* . . .) answer.

"Because God tells us to. That's why." (Insert smug glances at all students texting instead of paying attention.)

She sits back with a satisfied smile and a couple more points on the chalkboard, but in reality she's just repeating what she's been told. And anyone without their focus on a handheld device can do that. We don't need people who parrot Christianity. We need people who live it out. So, yes. The answer is correct, precious little wiggle-pants. But why? Why does prayer matter so much to God?

Because *relationship* matters to God.

Prayer is one of the fundamental ways we enter into a personal relationship with Him, and the great and beautiful mystery is that He desires that from us at all. If you really believe that God is all-powerful, perfect, holy, all-sufficient, and above every other thing, then you may be wondering why He *needs* us to pray.

Again, good question.

The answer? *He doesn't.*

He doesn't rely on our prayers to keep things running. But He wants them, because they are an indication of our heart for Him. Do you believe He is able to hear your prayers and to allow them to enter into a divine conversation with the living God? I hope so.

But listen.

That doesn't mean you have to understand the particulars of how it all works. I've heard people say they don't pray because if God already knows how everything is going to work out, what's the point? I don't actually disagree with the first part. I'm sorry if that makes you nervous. I quite like to think of the God I'm giving my life to as One who is all-knowing. So I will be up front with you in saying I don't believe our prayers can ever change the sovereign will of God.

Don't start with the robot thing, that's not where I'm going with this.

This is a hard chapter for me to write and I've sat on it for days. More often than not I've started to type what I'm about to share with you and I have decided to bury my head on the desk and then check Pinterest instead.

I think it's because I get so caught up in being misunderstood that I just decide not to say things at all. And the Lord has dealt with me on this as I've been working on this book, so at the risk of being seen as a freaky aberration of humanity (Drastic? But go with me. It's bound to be interesting at the very least), I will state my own perspective on the matter.

I believe God knows everything that is going to happen. I believe He has sovereign control over all events and circumstances and that nothing happens outside of His will. Quite simply, we just don't have that kind of power.

Here's where it gets dicey, right? Because if that's the case, why should we bother?

And Angie, are you saying we can't change God's "mind"? Because Abraham sure seemed to. Remember? He asked God to back down off of His plan to destroy Sodom if he could prove to Him that there were still a few righteous people there. And then

Abraham negotiated that number with God until God finally changed His mind. REMEMBER?!?!

I'm tracking with you. I've read those stories and I hear what you're saying. I just don't agree with the notion that Abraham made God act outside of His own will. So do our prayers have an impact? Yes. But often times, we are misguided in the way we measure "impact."

If we are going to the throne of God with the notion that something we persistently bring to Him can eventually (with enough tears, effort, and earnest begging) change what He has willed to happen, I believe we are wrong.

So do our prayers matter? My answer is an unequivocal, wholehearted, passionate yes, but as far as telling you exactly how the mechanics of time/space/human will/God's sovereignty thing works out, I'm more gray than black and white. And guess what?

The gray? *Is okay.*

(I didn't realize it was going to rhyme like that. Maybe this could be the bumper sticker we've been waiting for . . .)

At the end of the day, my desire to take apart the process of prayer boiled down to this: *What are my "rights"?* It was more about wanting to control an outcome than it was about wanting God. Bad idea.

And this is the nature of the God-chaser. We want to know we are the hunters and not the hunted, don't we?

Let me ask you this: Are you asking the "hard questions" because you want God to answer? Or because you want to hear your own voice? There's a difference, I'm afraid. And I know that from experience.

We tend to see things through our control-obsessed eyes and we feel life with hands that want to strangle everything that tries to squirm. We aren't equipped to do this. And we're in dangerous territory when we start feeling entitled to every detail of God's majesty.

We can wrestle it out and make a scene, or we can just admit that at the end of the day, our voice isn't the one that matters the most.

I didn't surrender because I was intimidated by the scholarly side of things, but rather because I grew tired of being so important to myself. So I told Him I didn't understand. And then I prayed like I never had before, with every assurance that the mystery is more beautiful than my wildest academic satisfactions.

I love the way R. C. Sproul explains it:

> When God sovereignly declares that he
> is going to do something, all of the prayers
> in the world aren't going to change God's
> mind. But God not only ordains ends, he also
> ordains means to those ends, and part of the
> process he uses to bring his sovereign will to
> pass are the prayers of his people. And so we
> are to pray.[10]

He tells us our prayers make a difference, and while they don't make Him reassess what He has ordained, it does mean that there is a dance we can't quite understand that happens. In that dance, He takes our hearts and our supplications into consideration, and they are important to Him.

Some prayers He may use to grow our faith in Him, and others He may allow to be a strengthening tool in our relationships with others. We may (and hopefully will!) see drastic answers to our prayers play out right before our eyes, but we should not view them as a shift in the ultimate plans of God.

The best way for me to come to terms with that is to remember that God isn't bound to time the way that we are and He is able to take all things into consideration at all times. It isn't as clear cut as "this happened and then this other thing happened as a result." I believe there are times He urges me to pray because He wants me to have the communion with Him as I enter a difficult season. We just can't take something like prayer and pretend we understand it and we certainly can't approach it in such an egocentric way that we miss the growth and other rewards He offers along the way.

That's a lot to take in at once, but I hope you'll let it settle in you for a while and see if it resonates. Ultimately, we know that God is working all things for the good of those who love Him (Rom. 8:28), and we have to come to a point where we can say, "I don't know how this looks behind the scenes, but I am acting out of obedience and waiting to hear Your voice in the midst of it. And, Lord, *that is enough.*"

Can I buy you a latte? Show you my extensive candle collection? I'm not that girl who is wiggly and prideful in her own confidence. I'm just saying He's God and I'm not. So some of what I spend my hours chasing was never meant to be caught and it's making a mess of what was supposed to be spectacular.

I'll just do my part and let Him worry about His.

Or, as any good mother would say, You just worry about you, hon.

I realize this is a rudimentary example, but the other day while I was praying I had the image of a human heart come to mind. I had been working through this chapter and it felt like a sweet way to remember my role regarding prayer.

I know a little about how the human heart works (cue sixth grade science teacher shaking her head from side to side and handing back another failed test. No smiley face, as you might imagine).

Basically, it's a pump, and each side works to receive and then distribute in order for everything to run smoothly in the body. I only know this because I have books and teachers and researchers to learn from. And that's fantastic, but every one of them will tell you that the heart itself has no concern for the mechanics; it simply beats.

I realized I wanted to see the whole body moving instead of just doing my part.

I wanted to know the ins and outs of what I was affecting, and a little diagram of potential issues headed my way would be awesome. I wanted the scientist's view. I wasn't given that, and it wasn't by accident.

What I have been given is the ability to take in and give out. I don't really understand the way it distributes itself throughout the body, or how it is that it comes back to me, but it doesn't keep me from doing what He made me to do. And it doesn't make me insignificant. It just means I'm not always in a position to see or feel my significance, so I choose to defer to the One who does.

Prayer was a pivotal part of Christ's life, and He made it clear to His disciples that it was necessary even for Him to have communion with Father God. Often He would go out alone and pray for hours, which stirred a question one afternoon as He was teaching the masses.

It was a question from an earnest listener who wanted to have the same kind of relationship with God the Father as Jesus did. Jesus gives the man (and us) a beautiful model for the way we should approach prayer.

Let's listen in as the Lord speaks, and allow the words to bring us deeper into a place of worship as we invite the living God to teach us what only He can.

CHAPTER 6

Our Father

If we are to pray aright, perhaps it is quite necessary that we pray contrary to our own heart. Not what we want to pray is important, but what God wants us to pray. The richness of the Word of God ought to determine our prayer, not the poverty of our heart.

~ Dietrich Bonhoeffer

P rayer is critical to our growth as believers, and it's one of two primary ways we experience our relationship with the Lord, the other being Scripture.

I realized pretty quickly that I was using prayer to "chase" God. I was never really sure I was doing it correctly and I almost always had not-so-great motives. As I started really asking Him what prayer was supposed to look like (instead of asking all the people who made me feel like I was failing miserably), He led me to His words in the Sermon on the Mount.

We don't know the name of the disciple who asked, but we hear his voice as he bravely inquires of Jesus. The Lord has just finished a time of prayer, and all eyes were on the one who took a chance and spoke up.

"Lord, teach us to pray" (Luke 11:1).

It should be noted that nobody (in any of the Gospels) ever asks Jesus to teach them how to disciple others. Nor do they ask Him to teach them how to perform miracles or how to be effective preachers. And yet they ask Him how to pray.

If our role is to constantly become more like Him, we want to model His behavior and His decisions, but in this case He was often gone for hours (even nights) on end where they didn't have the benefit of observing Him pray. It seems to me that they are essentially asking Him to reveal what it is that makes those hours so necessary to Him, and to help them see a glimpse of the power of prayer.

In English it's less than seventy words long, but it provides us with a beautiful structure for our own prayer lives. Jesus didn't teach them this prayer in order for it to simply be repeated, but rather to give them (and us) a model of prayer.

It's important for me to remember that, because I can be a little like a Pharisee when it comes to this kind of thing. Who am I kidding? It's not just "this kind of thing." It's every area of Christianity. And I'm not sure it's "a little" either. I'm not necessarily doing it to look religious or righteous, but I just can't wrap my brain around a system that doesn't have a clear set of "do this" and "don't do that" about every single area that might ever be encountered. I need to know that I'm hitting all my marks, you know?

You don't?

You never stress about that kind of thing?

Well, that means you probably haven't underlined much yet in this book and you can likely get a good turnaround price from a used bookstore. That'll probably be your best bet at this point.

I'll just go ahead and say it. I love this unnamed disciple. Thank you, Mr. Disciple, for being the one person who asked the question everyone else was probably pretending to know the answer to.

Don't beat yourself up if prayer doesn't come naturally to you, and don't get caught up in what everyone else is doing. This isn't something that should frustrate you or make you feel bad about yourself. It's an opportunity to have real intimacy with the Lord, and that's no small privilege.

It begins with a heart that is humbly seeking God, asking Him to teach us what we don't already know. We're acknowledging that it's going to be a process, and we're going to move forward a little and likely back again before we make real progress. That's the nature of being a disciple.

Because the Lord teaches this prayer both here and in the Sermon on the Mount, I will be using both to get to the heart of what He's teaching, and will note when I am quoting from one or the other. They only differ in a few words, and certainly not any that change the meaning of the prayer, so I will use whichever has the most information as we go.

Jesus doesn't waste a single word, beginning with the phrase, "*When* you pray . . ." (Luke 11:2). He's clearly saying this isn't an "if" situation we're talking about. It's not a suggestion; we're commanded to pray. So when? How?

Immediately after this statement, Jesus begins the actual prayer portion with a short sentence we often breeze past: "Our Father in heaven" (Matt. 6:9).

I've been able to recite this prayer for years, but I hadn't ever let it penetrate my heart, allowing the words to hold the weight in my life that they were intended to hold.

Even as we read "Our Father," we are urged to remember that we exist in a community of believers. There is an inherent humility in recognizing we are a part of the whole and not simply an individual whose life can be untangled from everyone else's. He isn't just my Father, but the Father of many, and my prayer and life should reflect that I am aware of that.

He uses the word *Father* intentionally, because in Jesus' day, most religious people had a notion of God that made Him seem distant, cold, even unreachable and fearsome. The biblical perspective of God is that of a Father who desires to give good things to those who love Him, and it assures us that He is trustworthy. He is our Abba Father, and because of Christ's blood, we can approach Him as such. It's an intimate term, reserved for those who have identified Him as our Savior.

One of the most striking things I read while studying prayer was that "In all His prayers, Jesus used the title *Father*, except when He was on the cross bearing the sin of the world and was forsaken by God."[11]

God is relational by His very nature—Father, Son, and Holy Spirit. Jesus took comfort and strength from being able to call on God as Father, so much so that in every prayer He acknowledged the Father nature of God. In the hour of His greatest agony, and in obedience to fulfill the path of redemption for us, even His Father turned His face from Him as He bore our sins. He was separated from God, bearing the full weight of sin so that we could forevermore call Him Father.

I often take that for granted. I don't think of the cost that came with opening the door to have relationship with Him. While we do have that privilege, and it's abundantly clear throughout the New Testament that we do, we also need to come to Him with reverence.

This is an important tension and one we will (or should) ever overcome because it's the nature of our standing with Him. He is our Father, but we shouldn't come before Him flippantly or more relaxed than respectful. It is intimate, yes, but our affections for Him are inextricably tied to His essence that is marked by a holiness we cannot fathom.

The phrase, "Hallowed be Your name" reflects that we come to Him in full recognition of who He is. Ultimately, we are coming to Him with an awareness of the fact that to be in His presence is a gift.

That's not to scare us into thinking we can't approach Him, or to make us question whether or not we are "good enough" to do so. This speaks to the attitude of the heart and a posture of reverence that comes naturally as we understand the character of the God we are addressing.

That's what hallowed means: holy. We glorify Him as we acknowledge this in the way we come to Him and, we put ourselves in a position where we can more accurately lean into His will instead of pushing our own agenda. For me, it's a moment of pause, where I can rightfully see the rest of my prayer time in light of the overarching truth—He is worthy no matter what.

And remember, this isn't a checklist. It's an attitude.

I know that it's easy for me to get settled into an entitled mode of thinking, where I end up rattling off all the things I want Him to do to make my life look different. They aren't always selfish, although often they are. When I take a few moments before beginning, and I let that reminder guide me, it's amazing to see how my perspective changes. *You are holy, God. I'm not. I'm grateful I can speak so easily to You, but don't ever let me fall into believing it's my right to do so.*

This leads us into "Your kingdom come, Your will be done," which is an indication that we defer to God in all matters. It is our way of saying that ultimately we want to be in the will of God in everything we pray about. We're going to get into this more in the next chapter because there are a lot of ways we can get discouraged and even feel helpless without a good sense of how our will and God's dance together. I'll go ahead and give you the conclusion in case you are going to hold your breath (which could be dangerous). I don't have a perfect answer. But I do hope to share a little of what gave me peace in the hopes that it might do the same for you. Sometimes (often) the dialogue itself gives way to a softening of the heart, and instead of holding out for an airtight solution, we learn that it's simply safe to rest in the mystery. So we'll dig into this more fully as we move on.

"Give us this day our daily bread." This is the part of our prayer, whatever the words we choose, that indicates our awareness of His provision in our lives and our dependence on Him for that gift. It's not just food we're talking about, it's all the things we *need*.

I love the fact that He uses the word "daily," because it reminds me that this is a *constant* prayer and recognition. We don't need to ask for more than today's portion, because we will pray tomorrow to ask for that same thing again.

It's like the Israelites receiving only the amount of manna needed to sustain them for the day. They had to make a habit of being dependent on God and were punished when they tried to stockpile it out of doubt.

Where do you struggle with allowing God to provide for you daily? What are the places that feel unsafe, where you are tempted to try and hoard what you can in order to protect yourself from potential drought? I can hardly think of an area where I'm not at least tempted to get ahead/gather up/form my own back-up plan and leave enough for another day. Whether it's money, emotional issues, or even housekeeping, I feel the need to have a safety net rather than trust God's provision. It's so silly, but I try and take control instead of allowing myself to rest and trust that He will come through.

It's as if I am saying, "Thank You for what You did today, but I'm not really convinced You'll keep it up, so I'm stepping in."

He asks us to have the kind of faith that wakes in the morning not knowing how He will provide, but believing that He will, based on what we know of His character.

I'm a whole lot better at typing it than I am at living it out.

We know what we need and He might be busy, so we'll go ahead and plan in the event that He's occupied. You can call it whatever you want, but the reality is that it's our lack of faith that causes us to act instead of ask.

He's a good enough Father to let us learn our own lessons, and trust me, this is one I have to learn over and over. I can exhaust myself running around like a maniacal squirrel, fully convinced that it is my searching that will keep me protected and well-fed. Instead of pausing to pray to the God who is in control of the whole universe, I scramble and gather, scramble and gather. And when I have a sufficient amount stored (according to my standards), I may go ahead and thank Him.

It basically means I say I trust Him but I act like I don't. Which is, you know, less than optimal.

It has only been with the benefit of hindsight that I have often realized how misguided my "solutions" were. I grew in the seasons where He didn't do what I thought was necessary for my well-being. I learned what it feels like to be infused with the hope that defies circumstance. While I can't say He's always done it my way, I will say He has always come through for me in a way that made Him more real to me.

The next portion of the prayer Jesus offered is twofold. We are asking for forgiveness and then recognizing that we also have a duty to forgive.

"Forgive us our trespasses as we forgive those who trespass against us" is at the heart of all prayer because it wouldn't even be possible for us to go to God if it wasn't for forgiveness. It's the foundation of our belief system as Christians and it's crucial to have awareness of what God has done for us as well as what we are expected to do in return.

Let's go ahead and say it: forgiveness doesn't come naturally to us as sinful, selfish people. There are plenty of times I come to Him with a laundry list of other people's offenses; He reminds me that I'm not really talking to a God unfamiliar with the concept of forgiveness. It's not that He doesn't care what you're walking through, or even that you have to edit your prayers, but it's a good reminder that we who are forgiven have been commanded to not withhold forgiveness.

And here's the truth. That person may really be wrong and you may really be right. But that doesn't mean you can choose unforgiveness as a valid approach. It's not an option for those who live forgiven by God. Does that mean you have to have a deep relationship with the person who abused you as a child? Absolutely not. And it doesn't mean you have to pretend it didn't happen. It simply means you are choosing to trust Him to bring about justice instead of believing that your resentment is valuable artillery.

He knows everything, so He will take care of things the way that are best as determined by Him. And that means that He doesn't need your sinful unwillingness to bring justice where it's needed.

> The one thing that is specifically forbid-
> den is vengeance, the very human longing
> to get back at someone. Perhaps you know
> the expression, "I want him to pay for what
> he did." How much passion there can be in
> those words! But getting even, paying back—
> vengeance—is territory that God expressly
> reserves for himself. "Vengeance is Mine, I
> will repay," he says. To try to get even is a
> dangerous business. We are playing God—
> stepping into a place that he claims as his
> own.[12]

We aren't ultimately responsible for what happens to the person we feel has wronged us and the best thing we can do is leave that up to God. The same God who decided you shouldn't be punished the way you deserved to be.

So there's that.

I'm not saying it's easy, because listen, resentment comes as easily to me as a hot mocha. I have to fight it daily. Often that means leaving things alone even when they don't feel resolved because I'm choosing to believe that He is fully able to understand the situation and what should happen much better than I ever will. We know when we are choosing not to genuinely forgive and we act like there's something delicious about keeping that away from the "guilty" party. We erroneously give ourselves a whole lot of credit in doing this and simultaneously distance ourselves from God. He is clear in Scripture that if we are harboring unforgiveness, we have put ourselves in a very precarious position to say the least.

Jesus is very strong in His teaching on this. In Matthew 18, He told a parable of a servant who owed a great debt to the king. No matter how familiar you may be with this story, I encourage you to read it again as if it's the first time and think about how clearly this speaks to God's expectation for us to forgive. When the man who owed the debt was called before the king and could not pay, he was ordered to be sold along with his wife and children to work off their debt for the remainder of their lives. He fell to his knees and begged for mercy and forgiveness. The king honored his request and sent him away with both his personal and financial freedom. And yet, as he left the very meeting where he was forgiven, he ran into another servant who owed him a very small amount of money, and he demanded that the man pay him immediately.

I'm sure you can already smell the irony.

When the man begged for mercy and more time to repay the debt, he denied him and had him thrown in prison. Apparently mercy is much easier to receive than it is to distribute.

The other servants went to the king after witnessing this, and the king was outraged. He summoned the man he had just forgiven and had him brought before him again.

"'You wicked servant! I forgave you all that debt because you pleaded with me. And should not you have had mercy on your fellow servant, as I had mercy on you?' And in anger his master delivered him to the jailers, until he should pay all his debt" (Matt. 18:32–34).

Calling someone wicked is pretty serious business. And in the event that you're not convinced of the importance of forgiveness, lean in and listen to the king's next words to his ungrateful servant. "So also my heavenly Father will do to every one of you, if you do not forgive your brother from your heart" (v. 35).

Yeah. It's not a vague suggestion.

We've talked a lot about motivation, and it's important to remember that our forgiveness isn't something we just do to be obedient or because we fear being the wicked one. It's for our own good, as are all of God's commands.

If we allow this "root of bitterness" to grow in us (Heb. 12:15), we are effectively keeping ourselves from experiencing the full relationship and privileges of being a child of God. It's a big deal.

When I forgive someone, it doesn't mean they aren't held responsible for their behavior. It means I am accepting that I am not the One who will hold them accountable, and that I defer to His judgment.

It's supernatural to forgive, and it's only through His power that we are able to do so in a manner that truly heals us. The only reason this is possible is through His tremendous grace for us, and without realizing our great debt to Him, I'm afraid we'll spend our lives measuring our perceived injustices instead of the reality. Once we step into a space with God that says (notice I didn't say *feels*) "You have forgiven much more than this, Lord," we are behaving like true disciples of Christ.

As D. Martyn Lloyd-Jones said so beautifully,

> I say to the glory of God and in utter
> humility that whenever I see myself before
> God and realize even something of what my
> blessed Lord has done for me, I am ready to
> forgive anybody anything.[13]

It certainly is a matter of perspective and one that changes everything. Who am I to withhold that which was unduly granted to me? Let that be the question that resonates within you when you're tempted to wield your own power instead of relying on His.

I love this simple explanation: "Forgiveness is looking the pain straight in the eye and saying, 'God is bigger than this.'"[14]

That's a good word right there. When I go into my prayer time, I continue saying that, asking Him to relieve me of my emotional need to "make things right."

You're bigger than this, Lord . . . help me loosen my grip and trust You with it.

In some form or fashion in almost every prayer I say, I land on the next statement in the prayer that Jesus modeled: "Lead us not into temptation, but deliver us from evil." Even when I'm not consciously aware of the wording, the cry of my heart is that the Lord would keep me from the sin I know I can't keep myself from.

We lament with Paul as he identifies his weakness, "For I know that nothing good dwells in me, that is, in my flesh. For I have the desire to do what is right, but not the ability to carry it out. For I do not do the good I want, but the evil I do not want is what I keep on doing" (Rom. 7:18–19).

Even where I have the will to walk in the ways of God, I don't have the ability to follow through. Maybe you're like me, and that statement feels a little like a trap when you first read it. Misunderstanding what the Lord is saying here could lead us to walk away seeing Him in a way that wrongly leads us to question His heart for us.

So, God set up the situation knowing that I would fail? Where's the compassion in that? I didn't even get a shot at doing it right!

I get it. But again, we're standing so close to the issue that we're forgetting the big picture. It's a fallen world, and we are fallen people (I mentioned this was a happy book, yes?) whose flesh fails in any given opportunity.

But.

(See! There's good news coming. Never fear . . .)

He has not purposed us to be robots (See! I told you we were NOT going there), constantly in motion in every wrong direction and steered only by the inherent redirection that comes with collision.

We do have the ability to choose, but there is no choice we can make that will supersede the highest call of God on our lives. No matter what we do, it cannot ruin what He has laid out for us knowing what our lives would look like. And as hard as that feels sometimes, it's also incredibly freeing to know we serve a God who loves us and takes everything and (eventually) packages it in a form of redemption we can't begin to comprehend.

Because we have His Holy Spirit empowering us, we can rely on that instead of our own strength. When we truly do, we are guided into a deeper life of godliness. The more we pray, the better we know the Lord, and the more clearly we hear Him speaking to us. It is this power that enables us to overcome our own selfish desires and poor decisions.

Even as a toddler, I was known for demanding my independence. My parents will tell you that when I was two years old I refused to let anyone else pass out candy on Halloween, screeching, *"ME DOOOOOOO!!!!"* when either of them came near me.

My husband, Todd, will tell you that my vocabulary has grown more substantially than my attitude.

I digress.

It's hard to recognize that you aren't the best person for the job when the job has been given the working title, "My Life."

And whether or not you choose to believe me, I'm going to go ahead and tell you what God has taught me over and over (And over. And then a couple more times.) about my life.

If given the option, I would have fished for hours in the dark. I would have despaired. I would have the best intentions, the sturdiest fishing pole made, a map of all the great fishing spots, and enough strength to reel in my catch.

But I would have come up empty-handed every time.

Not because I didn't know the water, but because I didn't know the Fisherman who created it.

Knowledge without power is just another empty net, friend. And He wants more from you. When we ask Him not to lead us into temptation and to deliver us from evil, we are saying that we recognize it's the only way it'll work.

Please, God, don't even let me have that as an option, but if it's Your will that I do, help me walk away and bring You honor.

Let me be sure that I'm being clear here, though, because it's been a source of confusion for many (myself included) at some point or another. Why would a loving God lead us into a situation where we didn't have the power to make the right choice?

Hear me say this loud and clear.

He wouldn't.

He doesn't.

He will never, ever, ever, ever do that.

Ever.

Are you picking up what I'm laying down here?

I sure hope so, because I'm running out of creative ways to say, "Not happening."

Scripture is abundantly clear on the matter—God will not put you in any compromising situation for which He doesn't provide a way out.

This reminds me of being on a cruise ship a couple of years ago watching a magician whose routine involved calling people out of the audience to put them on stage and embarrass them. It was all in good fun, but the fact of the matter was they could choose however they wanted from his deck of cards and they would still end up wherever it was he planned for them to. They didn't get an option because the deck was stacked. No matter how earnestly they tried, the outcome would be the same.

You aren't part of God's "shtick."

He always makes a way for you to do the right thing, and more than that, He is on your side. He wants you to choose well because He gets the glory when you do.

So the time when you lost your temper and said words you wouldn't dare repeat? Yeah, that was a choice.

The beautiful woman who started interning at your church and ended up having an affair with your pastor? There was another way.

The way you crave attention and seek it in the company of gin and tonic? He gives you a way out.

Don't ever catch yourself thinking for one second that God makes you sin, because it's more than a matter of semantics. He can't. It isn't in His nature.

And here is where we land on one of the most often misquoted verses in all of Scripture.

You and I have both heard it dozens of times, and maybe you've believed it yourself, but let's just set the record straight.

Are you ready? See if this sounds familiar:

God will never give you more than you can handle.

It's one of those phrases people pass around like an appetizer dish, nodding and inviting you to partake of the sentiment, and nobody dares to say it looks a little undercooked.

Listen. It's not only going to taste bad, it's dangerous. Stay away from the raw dish!!!

Here's the deal, friends. That little phrase is not in the Bible.

It's not a promise to hold onto or a reminder from the Lord for when we're up to our necks in difficulty. In fact, it's preposterous at best. So despite the fact that we've heard it as many times as other actual Bible verses, it's just simply not truth.

So, I guess you could say I disagree.

And you might also say I can be ever-so-opinionated. Which my parents and my husband would adamantly deny.

And then they would hand the Halloween candy back to me and life would continue peacefully in the wake of their grave error.

Anyway.

Come along with me for a moment as we head over to the text on which this often repeated statement seems to be based and see what it really says.

"God is faithful, who will not allow you to be tempted beyond what you are able, but with the temptation will provide a way of escape also, so that you will be able to endure it" (1 Cor. 10:13).

It's not talking about what you can "handle." Because quite frankly, everything in life is more than you can handle.

Which is why you need Him.

Are you still there? Okay, listen. It looks like it's bad news, but really it's not. And I wouldn't harp on a silly phrase unless I really felt like there was a good reason to have right-thinking, because your view of God is skewed in seeing the text any other way than what was actually intended.

He never gives you more than you can handle . . .

Which seems to say that if we have a lot going on, we must be pretty strong, right? No! NO! NO! NOOOOO!! RAW DISH ALERT!!

You don't endure pain or hardship because you're stronger than the rest of the pack.

You don't assume that God has given you a better grip on life because everything seems to be falling apart. God never says He won't give you more than you can handle. If you want to get technical about it, He actually says your life is going to have some rough patches. Like in John 16 when we are told that in this world we will have "tribulation."

Not "maybe," but "surely."

And not just trouble, but tribulation.

(Happy book, happy book, happy book . . .)

He's pretty up-front about telling us that things are not going to be easy and He should know. He walked all the same roads.

I don't mean to sound harsh here, because I don't believe the phrase was ever uttered to me in anything but encouragement, but it's just so inaccurate.

I was carrying a baby that wouldn't survive outside the womb and every day I had to face a new struggle as I dealt with the reality of loss. I chose a casket, a burial plot, a gown for her to wear when she was laid to rest. Every step was a heartbreaking battle, and when well-meaning people insisted I must be strong to have been chosen to carry such a burden, it made me sad that they felt this was true of the Lord.

The idea that someone would be faced with trial after trial because God believed they could handle it is depressing.

Friend, hear me. Please.

The notion that our Abba Father would dispense injury based on our ability to "carry it" is injurious to our relationship with Him and casts light wrongly on our human capacity instead of His generous dispensation of grace.

Go back. Read that last paragraph one more time like you have never considered it before. Because I believe that it is responsible for a good amount of our perception of God and it rests on boundary lines we have sketched in for ourselves. This isn't biblical.

Do not believe for one moment that the good and bad that happen to you is in equal proportion to how much you can handle without cracking. Because if we could do such a magnificent job of managing things, the sacrifice of Jesus would have been unnecessary. And I'm pretty sure that's not the angle we want to go with here.

Due to the fact that I actually feel the bottom of my feet sweating, I sense you may be able to pick up on my passion about this topic.

We are weak. We are dependent. We can't do anything on our own, and we aren't rewarded for our human efforts by another heaping pile of pain.

It's not His economy, and I for one am (obviously) grateful.

So, to summarize, yes. He actually gives us way more than we can handle in every moment of every day. But He also gives us Himself, which allows us to carry it at all.

I think we've got that part covered, so what is the Scripture actually saying about how we handle what we face? And how does that translate into our prayer lives?

What the Scripture does say is that He won't put you in a situation where you have no choice but to sin. He will never back you into a corner where you can't do the right thing. It isn't a matter of not giving us more than we can handle, but rather a reminder that God cannot make us sin.

For a long time I didn't understand the difference between "testing" and "tempting." I heard people say God didn't tempt people but He did test them and I felt like the difference between the words was probably negligible. I can tell you some amazing theologians to read if you want to dig into the depths of this topic—I'm not the one to do that. So I will give you my personal and practical understanding of the difference and you can either nod your head or send me nasty e-mails about how I have misrepresented the God of the universe in my ignorant thinking. Totally your call.

In order for me to reconcile the idea of a kind and gracious God putting His children in the face of potential sin, I needn't look further than the question that spurred me to write this book.

What is the motivation?

Is He doing it because He wants to dangle a chocolate bar in front of a woman on a strict diet and then laugh as she caves in just like He knew she would?

Shake your head. (The answer is no. I promise. I totally saw the answer key.)

Or . . . is it that He knows she has the choice to be obedient even when it's difficult and the glory of her obedience comes directly to Him?

And we have a winner, folks.

The former example presents an option that is sure to leave us weaker, while the latter reminds us that we can be strong in the face of difficult choices and become more Christlike in the process.

If you live your life as someone who sees God more like the first example, I don't blame you for being bitter. In fact, I would probably just grab the chocolate out of spite. Clearly I have a long history with sugar-related control issues.

But that isn't the case. He has given you the power to choose well, and He has given you the way out. Every time.

He isn't doing it to shame you, but rather because He wants you to be built up as you choose what is right and God-honoring. It is the heart of a Father who longs to see His children rise up and walk righteously.

It's the heart of a Father who believes they can.

Here is a profound summary that I came across on the difference between tempting and testing (but written by someone smarter than me):

> The former word conveys the idea of
> appealing to the worse part of a man, with
> the wish that he may yield and do the wrong.
> The latter means an appeal to the better part
> of a man, with the desire that he should
> stand. Temptation says: "Do this pleasant
> thing; do not be hindered by the fact that it
> is wrong." Trial, or proving, says: "Do this
> right and noble thing; do not be hindered by
> the fact that it is painful." The one is "a sweet,
> beguiling melody," breathing soft indulgence
> and relaxation over the soul; the other is a
> pealing trumpet-call to high achievements.[15]

If you think God is a carrot-dangling, deep-cackling dictator waiting for you to slip through a trap door, you can't possibly do anything but chase Him. It becomes a game of trying to outwit instead of resting in the love that says, "Pray for strength. I'll provide it in enough measure to get you out of this. But you're going to have to do your part, knowing that I'm doing Mine out of love and have given you everything you need."

The Lord's Prayer gives us a model of repentance, praise, and petition, but more importantly it gives us a glimpse into a conversation between a Father and His Son, rooted in a love that transcends words.

It's the raising up of a voice, the lifting of a heart, and the settling of a peace that ultimately comes from recognizing He is ahead and behind and above and He knows what we need more than we ever could.

Less than 70 words.

I'm bordering on 6,000 just trying to explain it.

Which, I suppose, is exactly the point.

I've chased God for a long while, which means I complicate things more easily than I accept them.

It was a good question, Mr. Disciple.

And now Lord, please give me grace to follow Your example.

CHAPTER 7

The Binder

Seek not to understand that you may believe,
but believe that you may understand.

~ ST. AUGUSTINE

I love learning. I appreciate the art of grammar and the philosophical arguments that lead me to think. I also love the beauty of literature, the art of structuring words, and the way it feels to stumble on something that feels significant. I am physically incapable of reading a book without a pen in my hand, and I've been known to cry in public, waxing poetic about the tragic circumstances in the latest biography I've picked up.

Life is my school and that means I'm always looking for ways to spiral-bind my circumstances.

In elementary school (and somewhat beyond—actually, way, way, way beyond) August signified one important truth. It was nearly time to choose the annual Trapper Keeper. I'm not going to explain the Trapper Keeper to those of you who are confused, because it makes me feel old. You are clearly a whippersnapper who has access to the Google and can search all of these terms on your own time. For right now, just know that it was crucial to school success—not just from an organizational standpoint, but also from a social angle.

It was also a huge commitment, and not one I took lightly. You don't just flippantly wander into Walgreens and pick the first majestically improbable theme you see, because it's going to be looking at you for the next eight months.

Two unicorns under a waterfall with an unlikely number of butterflies and breakthrough sunshine? It draws you in, yes. *But will it last?*

And there are always the kittens in a basket, which seem trite but at least they're not fictitious. They look so sweet, so cuddly, so, "Fifth grade is going to feel soft and loving if you choose us."

It's a lie.

Those kittens are a fuzzy invitation to the death of a status you have earned in years prior. Avoid eye contact with them. I speak from experience, grasshopper.

You might get more respect with the "pony alone in a field" option, or even the "heart-shaped-dolphin-embrace." This way you show them you have both feet on the ground but also appreciate creative interpretation.

And above all, you won't isolate yourselves from the solid-color team or the Lisa Frank crew. (←They can be an angry bunch. I can only urge you to make them your allies.)

I weighed my options carefully every year, begging my mother to drive me there before the only remaining choices were outer-space or sphere related. Because this "way more than a binder" binder was what was going to represent me, define me, identify me as meaningful and current, and also hold my stuff for the entire year.

In addition to the soothing "separating-velcro" melody, the Trapper Keeper offered me another chance at greatness.

There were no failed tests, no stories of hallway teasing, and no missed homework or messy handwriting. I took my time choosing and installing the loose-leaf paper, pencil pack, and tabs. I was selective about interior decorating, choosing only stickers that were related by theme and/or color to the cover.

Fine. Look away if you must. But let it not be said that I didn't take school (folders) seriously.

I liked it to look neat, because it made me feel a little more in control of an area that, historically, I had not been all that great at maintaining discipline. And every year, as I sharpened up my pencils and covered my textbooks, I imagined that this time was going to be different.

Potential always glows the brightest, doesn't it?

But eventually it loses its excitement, and we realize that no amount of dressing up can take away the issue that lies underneath. Until we are motivated by something that will outlive the annual Trapper Keeper, we don't have a chance of sticking with it.

If you work for the "Post-It" note company, you're welcome. I've kept you in business for the last few decades. I used to say I also kept the self-standing Blockbuster stores in business as well but it doesn't bear the same weight it used to. (Again, you spry little thing . . . don't remind me you didn't have VHS. It will get you nowhere with me. You're talking to a girl that watched *Punky Brewster* on BETA tapes. Yes. That was a thing.)

I love keeping track of progress. I love organizing and highlighting and writing on index cards and buying fresh, clean journals.

I love anything that looks like a door opening to faithfulness without requiring actual proof of commitment.

At this point, you're either confused or nodding your head, eager to see how I solved the dilemma you are currently facing.

Both parties would do well to contact my assistant at this juncture. I may have mentioned her previously. She will take care of your concerns and make sure you're satisfied with my foolproof approach to both (1) the seventh grade and (2) Christianity.

In the event that you fall closer to the nodding response, I first want to say this:

You are my people. Let's get together and organize something, all the while pretending we are going to follow through. The joy of life is found in a sharp pencil, and the world is our canvas!

We thrive on feeling like we can organize, structure, manage, and compartmentalize. We see the world as a series of hurdles we must conquer in order to be perceived as successful, and the Christian life is most certainly at odds with the majority of our other "teachers."

If you have been tempted to believe that you aren't smart enough to understand the Bible, I want you to hear me loud and clear.

He wrote it for you.

You don't have to have a degree, a literary bent, or even above-average intellect in order to experience God through His Word. For such a huge part of my Christian life I felt intimidated by the Bible. The problem with my approach to it was that I wanted to be a scholar and God never required that of me. I would rather steer clear of it than feel like a fool trying to comprehend it and then realizing I wasn't up to par.

Why was I chasing Him? He never asked me to.

God does not love Bible scholars more than non-scholars. (Scholars, we'll chat after class. Find something shiny and Greek for a few minutes.) He doesn't count the minutes people spend with their Bibles open in order to determine their heavenly rewards or their earthly influence. There isn't a magazine rack in heaven featuring covers of people who memorized the most verses.

I believe the enemy wanted to keep me feeling weak in this area because he knew that once I realized what God had actually offered me, I would be a force with which to be reckoned. And it wouldn't be because I could argue my way out

(But let's leave it nice and pretty and just talk about affectionate mammals instead of taking the chance we'll mess it up.)

So why would anyone with such immense affection for the structured start to do anything but open her Bible to Genesis 1:1, fully determined to make it the entire way through?

It was good for a while, because there's a lot going on in the first few books of the Bible. But then I got to Leviticus and it was slim-pickins as far as "wall art" options. I didn't make it the whole way through the Bible the first time I tried. Or the second. Or, I don't know, the first few dozen times. It's a little disheartening to feel like none of it makes sense but you don't really want to talk about it. Mostly because the people you might talk about it with often have "life verses" and that feels even more intimidating.

For the record, I still don't have a life verse. I don't know if that scares you or makes you want to stop reading, but I felt like I should come clean. It's hard for me to commit to a shampoo for a month so this just feels a little daunting to me.

Because I had virtually no exposure to the Bible before my adulthood, I didn't have any kind of framework for it. It was all so disjointed to me, and I knew I had to figure out a better way of understanding Scripture than just forcing my way through the chapters, ever mindful of the page count.

I decided pretty early on that in addition to reading small amounts of Scripture every day from my NIV Bible, I wanted something simpler. I bought a children's Bible and started making my way through that as well, and I can't begin to tell you how much it helped me. I realized that the stories I had read, the people whose names held no significance to me, they were intertwined. I began to develop a big picture view of the Bible, and eventually I was able to file things away in a manner that made more sense to me.

Every now and then I would be at a Bible study or church service and I would hear a certain verse and I generally (very generally, but still!) knew where/when/who it was related. It was exciting to realize I was learning, and while there isn't anything wrong with a healthy curiosity, I eventually came to the conclusion that I might be missing the point. I'm not going to say that's a theme of mine, but it could be. You might have picked up on that by now.

I wasn't going to the Bible to meditate on God's Word or to be present with Him.

I was going because I wanted to harness it, along with so many other topics I had studied over the years. It was another category that would make me smart; one that would allow me opportunities to share my opinion and feel relatively prepared to defend my beliefs.

I won't say that the Lord didn't speak to me while I read, because that wasn't the case. His Word is alive and active, and has the ability to penetrate the reader's thoughts, no matter the motive of his or her heart. But I didn't receive all I could have and it wasn't until some time later that I realized this very important part of my walk had also fallen victim to my "open and conquer" mentality. Over the course of several years, the Lord showed me where my errors had been in the way I came to His Word.

First of all, He didn't give it to me so I could build myself up.

I feel like I might be giving the impression that life is more about God than it is about us.

Let me rephrase.

I sure hope I am. Because like it or lump it, that's the case.

(Did I just say "like it or lump it"? I don't even know who I am anymore.)

When we are sensing ourselves becoming increasingly proud instead of humble, we can know for certain we aren't doing things according to God's standard.

I am not going to master the Bible. *Not ever.*

I'm not going to dissect every Hebrew verb tense or be able to close my eyes and trace the path of the Israelites through the desert as they wandered for forty years. Many people can do that and they may very well be the most godly folks you've ever met. But I can tell you with certainty and from experience that there is one motive that matters to God when you read His Word.

He wants us to know Him so we can glorify His name.

We live in a time period where intelligence and efficiency dictate our view of people's value. It's easy to fall into the trap of looking at self-growth as an objective in and of itself. In fact, it's encouraged. Pick up any magazine or take a look at a list of best-selling books and you'll see that the overarching message is "Make your life better. Take control and see results. Accomplish the impossible in 5 easy steps."

of a theological debate, but something so much bigger and infinitely more significant.

This Bible of mine? It is the breath of God spoken into my weary bones. It is the armor I need to walk the roads He has chosen for me, and it's the confirmation of promises that withstand the test of hours and adversity.

It's a love letter, and it has my name on it.

It has your name on it.

Hard to fathom, isn't it?

I believe that one of the most powerful ways the enemy has distracted us is by convincing us we aren't smart enough to understand the complexities of Scripture, and therefore, we won't get too much out of reading it. He wants us to feel like it's beyond our reach because he knows it's the best way to keep us weak and doubtful.

Here are a few other common excuses I've heard when it comes to reasons we don't read Scripture. (Make note of the fact that I am reporting my findings, NOT saying I am struggling with this. Because I am not. I am simply an objective reporter who has no personal experience with any or all of these issues. Carry on.)

"I'm too busy to read."

"I'm not smart enough to understand any of it."

"It's boring."

Again, these things were said by people who aren't as spiritual as me, and I just want you to know that it's out there. I don't get bored, distracted, or confused. A-hem. And "procrastination"? Is that even a thing?

So, now that we've got the basics on the table, let's see how we can make some progress.

Busyness.

Listen. I get it. I totally get it.

I have children.

A lot of children.

And I homeschool these children (if you are associated with the Middle Tennessee Home Schooling Association, I teach them exactly 180 days a year for a minimum of 6 hours a day). If you are not a part of that fine organization, let the record show that many days I have considered, "please go get my coffee" their home economics course for the afternoon.

Life is busy, and I don't want to paint the picture that I'm indifferent to what you have on your plate, but I do want to challenge you. If you live an existence where it is physically impossible to read your Bible for fifteen minutes a day, I think it's safe to say you might need to reevaluate your schedule. I don't have the margin right now to spend six hours a day holed up in a study pouring over Scripture, but I can certainly set my alarm a few minutes early and offer my intentionality and my full attention to reading the Word.

Yes, there are many days that I fall into bed and neglect to read a single verse. I'm not proud of it, but I want to be honest about my shortcomings. And I'm going to say something really harsh-sounding here (We're still friends, right, Lisa Frank-ers?) because I need to hear it as much as you do.

If we are choosing not to make time for daily meditation on Scripture, we are simply not convinced it has the power it claims to have.

Crickets

But it's the truth.

Know what I did find time to do today? Purchase two of the most perfectly mustard-yellow and white flowered pillows on the face of planet Earth. I stare at my bed everyday and lament the lack of "a pop of color." I reasoned that it was one of many things that would make my room a more inviting place, which would inevitably lead to more time spent there. You know, reading and pondering the words of God. In a roomy, soft, well-lit bedroom with a perfectly-placed (but not too intense, mind you. There's a balance here.) "pop" of color.

So, as you can see, I'm too busy securing the essentials for eventual success in my Christian walk to actually walk it now.

And surely that doesn't happen at your house, does it?

Which brings us to another great excuse.

"I'll do it tomorrow when I'm able to focus more."

If I could have majored in procrastination, I sure would have. And I would have been top of my class if that major actually had a graduation ceremony, which I'm kind of prone to doubt.

I would have minored in good intentions. Or, I would have earnestly planned on it.

I visualize it, I feel satisfied with the image, and then I settle back in to whatever I was doing because in some sense now I at least have a plan. And I tell myself that this time is going to be different. Because I have *a plan.*

A plan I might not ever execute, true, but the creation of it in my mind feels like progress. And then I just assume that at some point it will just go ahead and start.

Stop judging me.

You do it too, and if you don't, just pretend you do because I'm feeling fragile.

And truthfully, I have always chalked it up to being, umm, "motivationally challenged," but I have realized that's not actually the case. Which kind of stinks because the real problem is trickier.

I had an epiphany during a conversation recently and it challenged my understanding of my own procrastination. It isn't necessarily because I'm lazy or noncommittal, but more because I have an underlying desire to leave things as wonderful as they are in my fictitious creation of them.

It looks better in my imagination than it will probably ever look in real life, so I want to camp there and avoid the disappointment that's inevitable once I do something tangible. Don't you ever get so lost in your dreams about what could be that you stand still instead of stealing from the potential?

Remember the old Trapper Keeper? This is the equivalent of the sticker-choosing phase.

Make it pretty and worry about living it out later.

We so desperately want it to be exactly right that we would rather have a well-organized binder than a messy pile of effort.

And whether we call it procrastination, laziness, concern it won't turn out right, fear of failure, or anything else, we might as well also call it what it really is:

A form of doubt.

These excuses have some of their roots deep within another misconception about reading Scripture, and that is the idea that in order for Bible-reading to "count," we have to cover large chunks of it at a time, and that it all has to make perfect sense in our little brains.

Sometimes I feel like I need to read a specific number of verses before I can safely say I've done my duty as a God-follower. It's the classic example of imposing the world's view of "success" on a subject where it's irrelevant.

So in the event that you fall into this category, let me give you some breathing room.

God does not have a word count goal for you.

He wants your heart to be fully engaged and your mind fixed on Him when you read. He wants you to allow Him the opportunity to speak to you. What I found after years of reading the Bible was that I had stifled the opportunity to hear from Him by crowding my mind with facts.

My goal was to get a sticker on my eternal-rewards chart, so I finally read the Bible in three months. Even the parts about animal death, proper cleansing rituals, and creepy love triangles in the event that there was extra credit. (Again, smarties say this is a no-go.)

I wanted my bases covered. That was the objective. So I felt pretty accomplished when I got to the end of Revelation, but I wouldn't say the experience made me long to do it again. Basically I saw it as a hoop, and once it was jumped through, there wasn't a whole lot of logic in going back.

I'm willing to bet that at least some of what I've said so far has struck a chord with you, and if it hasn't, don't fret. I'm pretty certain I'll get there before we're through.

My motivation for reading Scripture was wrong, so the whole process felt like a burden.

And of course it did.

It's not supposed to be contained by the human intellect in its fullest profundity. It isn't a project to be aced. And if I go into it with an agenda or a feeling of obligation, I'm bound to end up frustrated. Additionally, "not being smart enough" isn't a valid excuse. He did that on purpose. You might not feel like you're smart enough to get as much as you want to out of it, but God promises you will get what you need from it as long as you are diligent.

Here's another bad idea. Get completely obsessed with drawing all of the maps on a wall and then placing small replicas of biblical characters all along it, quizzing yourself about the cities, battles, prophets, miracles, and so forth.

I'm just throwing it out there.

We come away most impacted when we go to Scripture wanting to gaze at Him, not search around for signs of Him. He is there. And if you haven't heard Him or been impacted by the Word, go back. Slow down. Listen.

For me, the chase gave way to abiding when I began to understand the difference between studying and meditating.

I was able to grow exponentially in appreciating the Bible—it became a gift instead of a duty. In fact, I felt emotionally connected in ways I never had, and I had a sense of awe that had been absent in prior times of reading.

I started with something that might strike you as elementary; I prayed that God would give me the desire to read the Bible.

I know. It's so crazy, right?

I heard Beth Moore talk about how she asked the Lord to help her memorize Scripture before she started and I flat-out shook my head and said out loud, "NO. WAY. This is genius."

Because clearly I have a lot of insight into why I'm failing.

I'm going to go ahead and tell you this and you are likely going to need to stabilize yourself. Take appropriate measures and then carry on.

It works.

Let the record show that I now realize how absurd it was not to pray. And let the record also show that I memorized the entire book of Hebrews in fifteen minutes. That last part is a lie, but the excitement took over for a minute.

So, here's what meditating on the Word looks like for me.

I don't wait for the perfect situation. I open up to a Scripture and ask for new eyes this time. I don't want to be so tangled up in my head that I'm not simply appreciating it for what it is.

It's the living, breathing Word of God. And I was treating it like advanced calculus.

I read slowly, and I don't beat myself up for reading only three verses if that is what I feel the Lord leads me to read. It's enough.

Then I go back and reread them again. And again. And again.

And listen.

I hear Him.

I surrender myself, wholly open to what He would teach me. And He does. Every. Single. Time.

Because it's not about me wanting to learn. It's about me wanting to be *taught*.

There's no cramming for an exam or worrying what the other students are up to. It's me and Him. And I'm beside myself that such a simple shift in my approach has done so much for my growth and love for the Word.

And for Him. Just love for Him.

Jean Fleming gives a beautiful illustration about meditation when describing an assignment she was given as an art history student.

> I was to write a two-thousand-word paper on a vase housed at the Baltimore Museum of Art. No research allowed, only observation. I remember circling the case, wondering how I could possibly say so much about this one object. But the more I looked, the more I saw. I scribbled notes about its shape, color, texture, materials. I wrote about the design

painted on it, the story that the scene might depict, how the vase might have been used in the past, how I would use it if it belonged to me. This is a process very much like Christian meditation.[16]

I do want to note that the meditation I am referring to is a biblical concept, and is not what Eastern religions mean when they use the term *meditation*, which encourages participants to empty their minds and create a space where they are completely passive in order to enter a higher or altered state of consciousness.

The Hebrew word used in the Old Testament for "meditation" refers to the word *muse* in its definition. To muse means to "turn something over in the mind—often inconclusively." Essentially, we are considering the words, allowing them to speak truth to us without allowing our primary goal to be academic comprehension and understanding. We meditate on Scripture by allowing it to soak in deeply and change us, not by actively pursuing a specific end.

There are many occurrences of meditation in Scripture, one of which is found in Joshua 1:8, "Do not let this Book of Law depart from your mouth; meditate on it day and night, so that you may be careful to do everything written in it. Then you will be prosperous and successful."

I found that when I approached Scripture this way, I was focused on Him and not myself (clue #1: I was on the right track). It became a fresh experience where I was constantly overwhelmed by the power of His truth. I stopped pursuing an end goal—abandoning agenda in favor of listening and believing He would meet me there.

And every time I finished reading, I realized that I left hungry instead of satisfied.

I wanted to do it perfectly or not do it at all. And I came around to the (crazy, totally unpredictable, unlikely, and altogether shocking) realization that, well, that's not a great way to approach anything, let alone God. No more excuses, no more chasing.

Meditate on His Word, and commit it to memory. This is our arsenal against the enemy and against all the trouble we face.

Motivation matters, though.

It's not about getting extra credit or looking smart in Sunday school. It's about knowing Him and loving Him in deeper ways. Put your full weight into the words, in full belief that they are the cornerstone of a meaningful life with Him.

And please, please don't think you're not going to be able to make sense of it.

I know what it feels like to be the only one thumbing through tissue-thin pages and asking Him to show me where I'm going. You're not the only one who doesn't understand the big words, the long city names, and the begotten of the begotten of the begotten who then begot.

To some, they are words. Just *words*.

And to them it's a monumental task to take it all in.

But to us, *they are everything*.

Which makes it a monumental gift instead, and one we can hardly wait to give away.

You might not realize it at first, but He will give you treasures in darkness (I'm not trying to pull a deejay stunt. That's actually a verse from the Bible and I'm fully aware.) when you spend your days looking. Not because you're trying to make a diagram for class, but because He loved you enough to share His words with you, and He promises you it's worth it.

He will speak, mark my words.

It might even show up *(dare I say it?)* in Leviticus.

---

* After the writing of this chapter, I decided the pillows were all wrong for the room. I can't find the receipt, so now I'm stuck with them. They stare at me, mocking me with their "not as subtle as I thought" mustard hue. And no. The irony is not lost on me. Contact my assistant if you'd like to purchase them.

CHAPTER 8

Name This Place

Providence is wonderfully intricate. Ah! You want always
to see through Providence, do you not? You never will, I assure you.
You have not eyes good enough. You want to see what good that
affliction was to you; you must believe it. You want to see how it can
bring good to the soul; you may be enabled in a little time;
but you cannot see it now; you must believe it.
Honor God by trusting Him.

~ CHARLES SPURGEON

I n retrospect I can see where I went wrong.

You'll have to believe me when I say at the time it seemed like a legitimate way to teach my children about meeting others' needs and having a sacrificial spirit.

In that spirit, I will now awkwardly transition into what will heretofore be referred to as "The great parenting fail of 2006."

I had been growing my hair for quite some time in order to donate it to Locks of Love, and the day of my appointment finally rolled around. I explained what I was doing to my twin daughters, who were five at the time, and they were very supportive. For the record, they were old enough to understand "haircut" and "unselfish," so I thought we had the basics covered.

Visions of "Mother of the Year" awards danced in my head as I drove to the salon.

My hair was barely long enough, so the hairstylist made two braids before she cut to make sure it would meet the required length. After she cut them, she slipped the braids in a little white envelope and I cried.

I wondered where they would end up and what the circumstances of that child would be. It was overwhelming. I started crying and I suppose it was the way I clung to the bag that led the woman to believe I was upset about losing my hair. She kept talking about what a cute bob it was going to be and I nodded, holding the bag against my chest while tears spilled on my plastic cover-up. I was so upset I never clarified and to this day she probably thinks I was just really attached to my own hair.

Sidebar: If you are that woman, I want to thank you for the adorable bob that you did indeed produce. I was crying about cancer, not my haircut. I apologize for traumatizing you with what must have looked to be an extreme form of narcissism. Love, the braid-clutcher.

I was probably still splotchy and red-eyed when I got home, which may have added to my reception, which was less than optimal.

Let me be more specific.

There was screaming and panic.

A lot of screaming. A fair amount of panic.

I should also mention that I share a trait with my oldest daughters that seems to have escaped the rest of the bunch. It's called "change is the scariest thing on earth outside of that one Disney movie with the deserted carousel that spun on its own and played carnival music."

At least, that's what we call it. You might have another name. Like, *The Last Unicorn*. Fill in with whatever appropriate kids' movie scarred you and/or your children.

I hugged them and assured them that everything was going to be okay—actually, more than okay! I decided (This is the next step in a series of bad choices. I realize that now.) that the best way to get them excited about the situation was to remind them of the good that was going to come from it.

And apparently the best way for me to approach this goal was by reaching into the white envelope and pulling out my braids, one in each hand, and holding them in front of the girls' faces. (I know. **I KNOW.**)

In my defense, I was saying things that made sense and could have prevented therapy, but evidently the high-pitched dog noises they were making hindered them from hearing me.

So I came up with a new plan.

I calmed them down enough to sit beside me as I searched online for the website. As the photos of precious little bald children popped up on the screen, I could tell that they were interested. And they weren't shaking in terror anymore, which felt like progress.

I reminded them why I cut my hair and told them that there is going to be a little girl smiling like the one in the picture when she got her new hair.

Then, Abby asked me if these children are going to die.

I wanted to tread carefully, but I wasn't going to lie, so I told her that I didn't know for sure. I explained that some of them might go see Jesus sooner than others, and that it is a hard thing for us to understand. I told her that's why I wanted to cut my hair and that we will pray for their health.

It seemed to click a little more and her face softened.

Ellie, on the other hand, buried her face in her hands.

And I presumed it was because of what I had just said, so I lifted up her little head and asked her if she was okay. Her face crumpled up and she started choking out words.

"But . . . Daddy . . . is Daddy . . . *oh, no . . . Daddy . . .*"

I was confused.

"What, baby? Honey, what's wrong about Daddy?"

"IS DADDY GOING TO GO SEE JESUS!?!?!?!?!?!" she shouted in anguish.

Now, listen.

If you don't know my husband, you won't have pieced this together yet. Here's the missing link: He shaves his head and is therefore every bit as bald as the sweet little pumpkins we were looking at on a computer screen.

And I realized that in her mind that meant he might die. Well-played, Mom. Well-played.

I explained that baldness does not necessarily mean cancer and that Daddy was not sick. I felt like a horrible person. (I hear you whispering. Understand that I GET THAT IT WASN'T MY FINEST HOUR.) I choked up again because I was telling them how grateful we should be because we do have our health and that we should thank God for it. Now I was making dog noises and they were just staring at me, confused and more than a little convinced I was in a dark place and probably needed some "me time."

I assured them everything was okay and they recovered and told me they actually liked my haircut. (See, hair lady? The kids even liked it! We're cool, right?)

Then I tucked my braids back in the envelope and put on an episode of *VeggieTales*, because it had become abundantly clear to me that at this point their best shot at learning life lessons was broccoli.

We are predisposed to see things from the angle that makes us feel the most vulnerable, and in Ellie's eyes this might mean her daddy wasn't safe.

I can't help but walk into situations asking, "Are You going to provide for me, Lord?"

It was another one of a long list of questions He needed to answer in order for me to say I trusted Him. I was so fearful, so consumed by my own lack of control, and so determined to make sure He was the faithful God He seemed to be for others.

He has promised to take care of us, to make good come of evil and to love us with indescribable fervor. But the six o'clock news makes Him look, at the very least, inconsistent. Maybe just flat-out untrustworthy.

The question "How can you say God is good?" has been posed to me more times than I can count and I understand the reasoning.

A few weeks ago, I visited the cemetery to be with my daughter on what would have been her fifth birthday.

I am, by all accounts, a woman who might have a hard time saying God is good. But I do.

With that said, God Himself knows that there are plenty of times when I question His plan and wonder why He allowed her to die, so there's no point in pretending I don't.

He has promised me He will provide what I need.

And when I say I believe Him, it doesn't mean we always agree on the definition of "what I need." It means I defer to Him, knowing that I'm seeing hair in a bag where He is braiding hope.

And one day I'll see the glory of it all.

———

Abraham was intimately acquainted with God.

He had been given the promise of generations as numerous as the stars and He took God at His Word.

Those words must have held Abraham through many seasons of doubt and loss, but none greater than the test he would be given when his son Isaac was nearly a grown man himself.

Like Isaiah, as soon as Abraham heard God's voice calling his name he replied, "Here I am" (Gen. 22:1).

He presents himself to the God he serves, eager to please Him.

And then God speaks words he never could have anticipated.

"Take your son, your only son Isaac, whom you love, and go to the land of Moriah, and offer him there as a burnt offering on one of the mountains of which I shall tell you" (v. 2).

A couple of things I want to add here (in addition to the fact that this is probably not Abraham's favorite morning).

The Hebrew words God is using to describe Isaac as Abraham's beloved son represent the same concept that would be used to describe Christ. He is Abraham's "only begotten son." In addition, this is the first time in Scripture that we see the word *love,* and it is used to describe the love a father has for his son.[17]

I don't know what Abraham felt in that moment, but if his actions are an indication, he was prepared for obedience. He rises early (Early. As in, "not procrastinating" and "not stopping at TJ Maxx for pillows.") the next morning to saddle his donkey and gather two of his men and Isaac, cutting the wood for the burnt offering himself. Typically, this would have been done by one of his servants, but not in this case. He does it himself, as if he's taking ownership of his responsibility.

And remember, he didn't know where he was going to end up because God hadn't told him, so he just begins walking.

I read this many times and somehow glossed over the fact that it wasn't like he walked for a half hour and then God pointed to where he should go.

Three days pass.

Sound familiar?

On the third day, Abraham "lifted up his eyes and saw" (v. 4) the mountain where he was to sacrifice his son. The Hebrew word used here is *ra'ah,* and it means "to see, to look at, inspect, perceive, consider."[18]

He told the two men that he and his son were going to go there, and told them that they would be back. Not *I* will be back; *we* will be back.

Some suggest that he didn't think God would really ask him to kill Isaac and that's why he was confident about saying they would return together, but Hebrews 11 makes it clear that Abraham knew that God was able to raise Isaac from the dead. I personally believe he did think he would have to offer his son, but he trusted that God would keep His promise and would therefore bring him back to life.

As a result of that faith, he and his son go and worship before continuing.

Worship.

It's the first time the Hebrew word that most clearly translates to "worship" is used in Scripture, and what a profound place for us to learn what it looks like to express praise in spite of circumstance. Circumstances are unrelated; God is worthy of our praise in any situation.

I'm sure you can see the foreshadowing of the coming Christ in these verses, but it's especially profound to consider what happened next, as Abraham laid the wood on Isaac. Like the Lord to come, Isaac would carry his own wood to his death.

Isaac saw there was no animal for the sacrifice and inquired about it. His father assured him that God would provide, and that seemed to be enough for Isaac. In the next verse it says they went together, and it isn't just referring to the fact that they walked side-by-side. It means they went in agreement.

I don't know when Isaac realized (or was informed) that he was going to be sacrificed, but it's clear that he accepted it on the same faith as his father. After all, Abraham was an elderly man and could hardly have kept his son on the altar if Isaac had fought him. Yet we see, even as Abraham bound him, he wasn't struggling to get loose or even questioning the situation.

As Abraham lifted his knife in the air, an angel of the Lord cried mercy.

"Abraham, Abraham!"

I can't imagine any other response such a man of God would have but the one Abraham offers yet again.

"Here I am" (v. 11).

Here I am, Lord. With my arm raised and ready to take the life of the son I love if You should say the word. Not because I understand it, or because it makes sense in my head, but because You told me to and I trust what You know more than what I can see.

What a relief must come to the father and son as the Lord told him not to harm the boy, acknowledging that he must fear (awe, reverence) God in order to have been so willing.

At that point, Abraham "lifted up his eyes and looked" (v. 13). He saw a ram caught in a thicket behind him and knew that this had been given as a substitution for his son. The word used here is the same as before, *ra'ah*. He lifted his eyes and saw what God was providing.

He took the ram and sacrificed it, naming the place "Jehovah Jireh," or "The Lord will provide." Verse 14 continues, "It is said to this day, 'On the mount of the Lord it shall be provided.'"

And I can't help but tell you what my human nature said in response: *Of course he named it that. He got to keep his son.*

God did provide for him. *But what about when He doesn't?*

I daresay I saw provision differently in the salon chair several years ago than the child who received her wig from my haircut.

It's easy to call it provision when you offered to give but nothing was really taken.

Would I say the same with my knife held above my head? Here I am.

Here am I, Lord.

I say it more than I mean it, and more often than I care to admit, I'm saying it while trying to hide. I don't want to be chosen for this particular activity. Go ahead and pick someone braver and it'll all work out in the end. I'll just botch it up anyway.

And underneath it all I'm really saying I can't promise I won't run. I am not one of those people who stand in the face of a crisis and worships. I'm not.

But He is, and He does it for me when I can't.

When I sat beside my daughter's grave, I was angry. I was devastated. I was everything you would imagine I would be as other moms were getting swimsuits ready for another summer and I couldn't do that for her.

There is nothing I can do for her.

And I want her here. Every single day, I just want her here.

So I sat with her on her birthday and I grieved the loss of her deeply.

But I loved Him there, just as I love Him in the rest of it.

And there came to me the sound of a question that I had to answer. It whipped through the wind as the tears fell, and I knew He was asking.

What will you name this place?

I didn't know what to say.

Jehovah-Jireh? The place where He provided? *Is it?*

How do I look at a birthdate on a tomb and call it that?

There was no thicket. No substitute. No ram.

There was a headstone covered with weeds.

And what, love, will you name this place?

The words didn't come from my emotion, but they fell from my lips because I believe Him.

I will call it the same.

This is the place where the Lord provided.

I don't know how or what or why or even really humanly understand that He did provide, but He says He did. So in this moment, I will echo His promise while the dirt stains my knees and the trees bloom life in the face of death all around me.

Later I went back and read the account of Isaac again. And I felt an urging to continue reading it over and over. I had a sense that He wanted me to see something I hadn't before, so I lifted my eyes.

Again and again and again. Listening as He guided me, truly believing He was speaking and desiring to know what He would have me learn in that moment.

And that's when I saw it.

I have read that story at least a hundred times, but had never noticed what became a monumental difference in my faith walk.

I can only tell you that when I read the words, I trembled.

Because in retrospect, I can see where I went wrong.

As Abraham and Isaac climb the mountain, Abraham assures his son with the words,

"God will provide for himself the lamb for a burnt offering" (v. 8).

That was the promise.

Not a thicket.

Not a ram.

A Lamb.

The Lamb.

He is a God who cannot break His word and around two thousand years later, God would provide exactly that.

Our perfect, spotless Lamb, who came to swallow our sin and provide our eternal security.

He was the promise, and the promise was kept.

I want you to stare at those words and let Him speak to your weary soul—you who are sure He has forgotten you and given up on what was guaranteed to you. Because the enemy of your soul wants you to believe that He doesn't care, that He doesn't hear you, and that He is not trustworthy.

It's what was behind the very first question Satan posed in the garden, and it remains in every situation we face today: "Are you sure?"

And the problem I faced in answering was that I was looking in the wrong direction.

My eyes were locked on a thicket instead of a cross.

I was relying on a promise He never made me.

And even when it feels hollow, I force the words because I know there is power in the truth. Satan comes in the most broken moments and he whispers lies and asks me if I'm sure God is for me. Am I sure He is good? Am I sure He provides?

There is power in truth, and I shout it with my soul—No. I am not sure about the ram.

But I am certain about the Lamb.

The enemy of my soul will not convince me that my circumstances reflect the way God is providing for me. It is simply not so.

He is Jehovah Jireh, both at an abandoned altar and at the cemetery gate.

This is the only time the phrase Jehovah Jireh is used in all of Scripture, and in the event that you want to know what Abraham really named that place, I'll tell you what the Greek word means. Or, you can do it yourself, because you already know the word:

Ra'ah

It has been translated to mean "provide," but in its essence, it really means that God "saw" Abraham's situation. And He sees yours. Right now.

When we wait for God to provide a ram before we will trust Him, we are missing the gift He has given in the Lamb slain for us. Provision doesn't mean it will work out here; it means His blood will make it right in the end.

I will lift my eyes and behold Him instead of chasing the words He never spoke.

It is in this place I learn to abide.

Whether my knees bend on soft grass or the cold dirt, I resolve to worship Him. The words are frail but sure, and they remind me that nothing has escaped His notice. It all rests in the hands that stretched east to west on a hill high above Calvary.

You see me, Father. And I thank You for it. You didn't have to make the trees bloom that day, but You did. I saw them in their splendor, after everyone told me they hadn't burst into flower yet. And later I would cry, not for the loss, but for the way You assured me of redemption. I saw it, Lord.

I know Your eyes were on me as I walked barefoot on the ground, looking up and seeing myself in the shadow of the cherry blossom.

And You knew I would stare at the ground, watching my dress whip around my legs while the petals fell. And that in that moment, I would know the shelter of providence itself. And that I whispered, where no one else could hear, *"Let me never forget this place . . ."*

Remind me, Lord, when the days grow long and my heart breaks over it all. Remind me that I stood still for the first time in a long time, and that You met me there. You knew, didn't You? Of course You did. You knew I would see the shadow, and that I would see You in the midst of the sadness. *You love me enough to do that.*

And You knew what I would say next, because it was impossible not to.

What else could I do but bow?

Here I am, Lord.

Here am I.

You have provided for me, and my deepest desire is to thank You no matter where You bend my knees.

CHAPTER 9

The Ink

And you show that you are a letter from Christ delivered by us,
written not with ink but with the spirit of the living God,
not on tablets of stone but on tablets of human hearts.

~ 2 CORINTHIANS 3:3

H e healed the boy . . . *He healed the boy!!!"* Shouts went
out and the word spread through the small town as
a boat drifted out into the Sea of Galilee in the black night.

As the story continued to be passed from person to person, eventually it came to a woman who had essentially been
in hiding for the last twelve years.

"He healed the boy with a demon . . . *He is a healer . . ."*

When I read Scripture I always wonder about the in-between
stories. For example, we know she must have been told, and that
she had enough belief to lead her out into the open, but we don't
know what it was like when she heard the news.

After all, she hadn't been considered "clean" for more than a decade, and with the constant bleeding she wasn't allowed to be in public. In fact, she couldn't even touch another person, whether it was her own child or a complete stranger, for fear that her disease would make them unclean as well.

She was an outcast in every sense of the word and I imagine she had come to accept that this was her lot in life. The loneliness was unfathomable, and the shame unbearable. When a woman was having her monthly cycle, it was seen as a time that the Lord was "purging" her of uncleanliness, and as a result she had to stay away from others. But in this case, it had gone on for years and years with no end in sight.

The Gospel of Luke tells us that she had spent her life savings on physicians, but no one could cure her.

But when she heard of a man who had come into town and performed miracles, I wonder if her heart jumped, knowing this might be her chance. It would be a brave thing to venture out into the open, but at this point it doesn't seem like she had much to lose by trying.

The whole town appears to know He would be coming back and they gathered on the shore in anticipation. Among the crowd stood the woman, likely trying to keep herself unidentified in light of her condition.

As soon as Jesus got out of the boat, a synagogue ruler made his way to the front of the people and fell down before Him, begging Christ to save his daughter.

"She's my only daughter. She's just twelve years old, and she's about to die. Please come and save her . . ."

I imagine the crowd made it easy for Jairus to get to the Lord, because he was such an important man in the religious community.

But the woman, not even able to enter a synagogue, hadn't heard the Word of God in years. The scrolls were kept locked up inside the temple and she obviously wasn't welcome there.

Who was she to think she deserved a blessing from the Healer? She knew better.

But the fact of the matter was that she believed He could heal her, whether or not she deserved it, so she did what she thought was best. She waited until Jesus was close enough to her, and coming from behind Him she lurched for the hem of His robe just to touch it.

On a priestly robe, there were tassels in each of the four corners to remind the wearer of the law and his responsibility to keep the commands of God. In fact, the Pharisees would make their tassels extremely long to give the impression that they were "holy" people. When Scripture tells us she reached for the "fringe" of His garment, this is what it is referring to.

As her fingers wrapped around it, I can imagine that she felt the bleeding stop.

Stop.

In an instant, the Healer's power had done what no physician could, and she knew immediately she was well.

And that was what she came for, after all. To just simply be made well. And that being the case, I imagine she felt her interaction with the Lord was over.

It wasn't the case.

"Who was it that touched me?" He asked.

Everyone denied it, including her.

The disciples asked Jesus how they could ever identify one specific person in a crowd that was pressing up against Him, but He didn't relent.

"Someone has touched me, for I perceive that power has gone out from me" (Luke 8:46).

She knew she had not escaped His notice, so she came forward, trembling.

Keep in mind that Jairus is frantically waiting for the Lord to continue with him in order to get to his daughter before it's too late. Jesus had something else in mind.

As the woman explained her condition in front of the crowd, I'm sure she was humiliated. She didn't want His attention; she just wanted to be well. And now all of these people would know what brought her here and they would likely judge her for what was considered a reflection of an unclean heart. She was useless and she was in the way of a more important cause.

She explained to the crowd that she was miraculously healed the moment she touched His robe and as soon as she finished telling her story the Lord replied, "Daughter, your faith has made you well; go in peace" (v. 48).

This is the only time in all of Scripture that Jesus calls a woman "daughter." And it's this woman—the one who thought the best she could do was sneak a blessing from the holy man. He was making it clear to her and to the rest of the people listening that she was one of His, and not only that, but she had been healed because she believed He could heal her.

Jesus didn't call her out of the crowd to embarrass her or to shame her; He wanted the crowd to understand that it was her faith, not her fingers, that had made her well. Furthermore, I believe He wanted them to know that she was considered healed, and that they should treat her as such.

In a time when so much emphasis was put on rituals and rules, the Lord was making it abundantly clear that there was nothing magical about touching His garment, nor was it something she physically did that brought her health.

In fact, the Hebrew word Jesus uses for "well" in this verse is *sozo*, and it has implications of eternal consequence; He is saying her faith has saved her. She is right with God, and she can go in peace knowing that is the case.

In the meantime, Jairus received news that his daughter had died, but Jesus continued on with him, urging him not to fear, and upon arrival at Jairus's home, Jesus raised the girl from the dead.

Jesus didn't need to be there to heal the little girl, and the woman with the issue of blood didn't need a firm grip to be made well. But the perfect God honored their imperfect faith in accordance with His will for them. We can't do it perfectly, but He can. And He will use what we offer based on what He knows of our motives.

For many years, I read about the woman and it never struck me that I think of Him a little bit like she did.

Who am I to think I have a right?

I'll just try to avoid His gaze and hold tight when I can, and maybe all will be made right.

I'll chase Him until I can get my fingers to reach just a sliver of His clothing and I'll pray it's enough. After all, it's the only way I can get to Him. I'm not a leader, a well-respected citizen, or a religious hero. I'm a woman with a past and I won't waste my breath trying to declare my innocence.

A child of twelve? What has she done? She's at an age where she's about to be married and she has her whole life ahead of her. That's the kind of person who deserves to be saved.

What it will take on my part is effort. And just enough desperation to take a chance.

So I chased Him.

And as I came to a point where I could hardly do it anymore, He reached me with His tender truth.

I hope you'll let Him reach you too.

You didn't catch Me, child.

Let go of whatever gave you the impression you could.

The truth is simple, and it will change everything.

I chose you.

You weren't another face in a sea of thousands.

You are my daughter.

And you are well because you believed Me, not because you reached Me.

Before the beginning of time I saw this crowd, in this town, in this moment.

I saw a woman who would be healed, even though nobody else believed she was worthy of it, including herself.

How many years will you go on believing it's you and not Me?

And how long will your fingers be so tangled in the law that you can't live out of My grace?

Because I wanted to hide. I wanted to do what everyone else was doing and live a life that pretended not to need grace.

I wanted to be able to run.

Because in order to tell the crowds I was healed, I would also have to tell them what I was healed of.

I wanted to know I could use my own strength to get somewhere that mercy might not reach.

And for a time, I believed I needed it.

It's the mentality of someone who sees God as a Master instead a Father, and herself a slave rather than a child.

It's the voice that nags from the pit. *He would never love you like that . . .*

Go on.

Run.

And maybe one day you'll catch enough of Him to heal.

───────────

He was a righteous Jew, and had made his way back to Jerusalem in order to celebrate Passover. He had no idea what all the commotion was, but he obviously got close enough to see what was happening.

As he stood at the edge of a rambunctious crowd, he saw a man making His way up the hill, a cross on His shoulders and a crown of thorns cutting into His sweaty skin.

He was agonizing as they taunted, struggling underneath the weight of the wood.

And before he could fully digest the scene, Simon was plucked from the masses and ordered to help this guilty man as He continued to His place of execution.

There are only two times we are told that someone is "behind" Jesus. The first is the woman with the issue of blood, and the second is Simon of Cyrene, carrying the cross behind the King of all kings.

Carrying the cross that would eventually bring His death and our life.

Simon wasn't a disciple of Christ's, and it's not likely he even knew who He was. He was just one man, in a crowd, who thought he might escape notice. And as his hands lifted the beam, I wonder if he saw himself as a victim. Wrong place at the wrong time, and nothing more.

It's unclear whether Simon was carrying the entire cross, or whether the crosspiece was still on Christ. It's likely the latter, possibly done out of frustration by the Roman soldiers who wanted Him to get there more quickly. Maybe the end was dragging as He went and they pulled a man out to lift it up and speed the process. It was customary for a victim to carry His own cross, so it's possible that this kept the weight of the cross on Christ, but a portion was granted to another person for some distance until they had reached Golgotha.

What a horrific responsibility. To walk in the bloody footsteps of a man about to be executed, all the while painstakingly trying to keep balance and not succumb to the intense physical agony. Step after step, seeing enough of the man ahead of you to know there is life in Him now that will soon be snuffed out.

In what we can piece together in the remaining narrative of Scripture, Simon carried the cross to the place where Jesus was crucified, and while we don't know the specifics of what he saw, we know he saw enough to believe Christ was the Messiah. He returned to his tiny hometown, where he informed his family of what he had seen and they too believed. From there, a church began in Cyrene, and one of the members from that church would eventually gather with others in sending Paul and Barnabas on their missionary journey years later.

We learn that Simon's wife was like a mother to Paul, and he sent his greetings to her and their family in the book of Hebrews.

So let me ask you this:

Was he randomly chosen from the crowd? Forced into submission by an angry officer?

Or could it be that before there was time, God saw this town, this crowd, and this moment?

I daresay we safely assume the latter. Not just with the bleeding woman or the man visiting for a time, but for every one of us.

And we have, then, a question that must be answered before we can know how to walk with this God.

Will you chase Him out of your own doubt, or bear His cross from the faith you have to offer?

Jesus said that in order to be His followers we must be willing to carry our own crosses, and there is a detail of that statement that we might skip past and not take to heart. These crosses are chosen for each of us, tailored to our lives and designed with the intention of bringing us as close as we can to our Savior.

As John Calvin explains so powerfully, "Though God lays both on good and bad men the burden of the cross, yet unless they willingly bend their shoulders to it, they are not said to *bear the cross;* for a wild and refractory horse cannot be said to admit his rider, though he carries him. The patience of the saints, therefore, consists in *bearing willingly the cross* which has been laid on them."[19]

It is the hand, steady on the beam, bearing the weight He allows us.

It is the faith, unsteady on the hill, longing for the day when we no longer feel the stabbing pain that reminds us we are pilgrims.

It is the truth that sets us free when we can't see an inch past the rainy dashboard window.

If He has purposed for you to bear a particular cross, no amount of stumbling or questioning can take it from you.

You have no more ability to drop it than you do to carry it.

I have spent enough time chasing God.

I don't need to know everything.

And that means I have to let go.

And keep letting go.

I wanted one more book to tell me He was good. A couple stellar sermons that made me believe He was reliable. What I had failed to realize for so long was so elementary that it startled me.

What I called running toward Him was actually my way of avoiding standing still where He was.

Because it's not always easy to find yourself in the hands of God, and I'm the kind of girl who likes to know I can stop for a fountain soda. The idea of God always seemed to be more of a trap than an adventure. And in that scenario, my only hope was to rely on my own powers of persuasion in matters where I felt a need.

I feel like I need to assure you that I didn't set out to write a book about my struggle with God that had approximately 1,000 words dedicated to my mother wanting a coke. And if you feel like this negates my ability to impart wisdom, I accept your concerns. But if you're willing to see it through with me, I hope it'll land in a place that speaks to you.

I bet that you've had at least a season (a lifetime? at least a moment?) where you saw your journey with God the same way.

Tight space. No say in direction, movement, speed, or ability to brake on a patch of ice.

And based on the limited amount of what you know is expected of you as a Christian, you believe you're supposed to be singing hymns and reciting your life verse (good for you, friend. Good. For. You. Put it in your Trapper Keeper.) over and over while you count the yellow lines. In your mind, He may very well be all of those things people have told you He is, but you can't help but feel more like a prisoner than a daughter.

This is what it feels like to chase God.

And for me, there was a moment in time where I felt like exiting the car was my best chance at happiness. I hit a rock-bottom moment where I essentially told Him as much.

I want out.

You win.

I'm too this and too that. I'm a control freak. I'm angry at the people who think this is fun. I don't really know You and I don't know that I want to. I just want to open the door, set my own feet in the grass, and walk. Enough.

I felt it all unraveling, and the scariest part was that I couldn't convince myself I cared. All I could see was the horizon and enough of Him to know that while He might be real, He wasn't safe. It's the only part of Him we can see when we're chasing, and it isn't enough to make us want more.

I won't tell you that I heard God's voice say these words, because I didn't, but I hope you believe me when I tell you I knew He was speaking.

I was fumbling for the door handle, desperate for a way to make sense of my own hurt, and completely unaware that I had missed the point.

And then He explained.

You've made an assumption, love. And it's one that will keep you blinded to My ways for the rest of your life.

What, Lord?

What makes you think you understand thirst at all?

Of course I do. I know what I feel, what I want, what I need, what is best, what is important, what is . . .

My fingers began to pull on the handle, tears stinging and heart pounding.

I was livid at the suggestion, torn into a million pieces at how misunderstood I felt by God. I felt like He was questioning my own ability to see life, and my instinct was to rebel. How dare He? And what does that even mean? Of course I know what thirst is. And I want out. But His mercy didn't allow it. His tenderness overwhelmed me, and I allowed it to.

I believed that what I felt was thirst. Or sadness. Or betrayal. Or any number of other emotions that tell me I have a need that isn't being met. It's my subjective reality of life, but listen, it's all I've got. And from this angle, it looks a little hopeless sometimes.

It took me awhile to pry my fingers off the door.

Because I had been running after Him for as long as I could remember, and I didn't know how to stop. I have given days of my life to the notion that I had some power to catch Him. And I couldn't help but hear His voice in the midst of it, urging me to see the truth. And in time, I began to understand what He had been whispering for years.

You chase Me because you trust your own legs more than you trust Me.

You chase Me because you can feel the air in your lungs, not because you want to breathe true life.

And as long as you can chase, you still get a say. You maintain part-ownership of our relationship. You would run forever in the wrong direction if it meant your flesh didn't have to admit the truth.

You chase because it makes you feel like you can.

And indeed, I did.

But not unlike the man who wrestled under the weight of the Lord's cross, I realized that my walk with Him is one of surrender, not a game to be won.

I wasn't there alongside Simon that day, but I know what happened.

He saw the light of the world extinguished and he knew he was the reason.

And some time later, he saw the light come back.

And he knew that God was the reason.

What other option is there when you have been chosen by the One who bears your crime, your illness, your sin, your shame, your doubt, and your pride? What option is there when you see mercy swallow the grave? When a pile of linen is folded in a tomb, the stone rolled away, and the dawn of a new day blinds you to anything but His love? What option is there when you know very well that the conditions were all wrong for fishing that day, but you cannot deny the net? When the waves that almost killed you can't keep His feet from walking?

What then?

I can tell you my answer, but it won't get you where you need to be. Because I am one person in a crowd of thousands and you are another. Each of us has a cross to carry, a journey ahead, and a lifetime of following the One who beckons. The years have changed, the course looks different, and the days are steeped in confusion and fear, but the promise remains.

Come with Me . . .

And you will see.

The books are fine, I decide.

They are others' words, others' assumptions, and others' theories about the God I follow.

But they are no longer stairs of pages leading to an unknown Father. They are, at best, a place to rest at the end of the day and stare up into the heavens He created. I cannot climb them and I'm not supposed to. The highest ceiling is unreachable by foot, or finger for that matter. It's faith that sees the heavens, not because of the man-made cathedrals, but in spite of them.

It's the reason I wanted to write this book in the first place, because I sensed that I was missing the mark a little and it was starting to affect the way I lived out my faith. And the truth of the matter is that I started writing it a year ago, but couldn't seem to make any progress. It wasn't for lack of trying—I stared at my computer, read books on spiritual discipline, and prayed for God to give me words.

What He was trying to tell me is no different than what I am trying to tell you, and the very methods I was using to write a book about following God were indications that I was still chasing Him. For the life of me and despite numerous deadlines passing, I could not come up with a table of contents. In fact, when my publisher asked me to explain the concept of the book I would choke on my words and point at shiny things.

I had the title from the beginning and I knew where it would end. As for everything else, I was at a loss. I am a methodical person in general, and writing is no different. But this one just would not come to me, no matter how hard I tried.

And therein lay the problem, only I couldn't see the forest for the trees.

It's actually laughable now. I have to be the only person in the history of the world that couldn't figure out why chasing after God was not the best method for teaching people how not to do so.

Maybe I should have stuck with the pixies after all.

Sigh

I'm appealing to you as a sister here, because what the Lord taught me over the last year or so has radically altered the way I experience Him. My deepest desire is for you to feel the same when you finish reading. Not because of this book, but because of His.

It has a title and it has from the very beginning.

And as sure as the dawn it has an ending.

The table of contents is not for you (or me) to write, and attempts to do so may distract us from the actual task.

The more I fight to fill in what He has left blank, the more I resist His sovereignty and indulge my own perceived rights. I don't need to know all of it in order to love Him and be near to Him.

I remember the day I decided to become a writer.

It was a good day.

Even better was the day I realized my pen held nothing but ink that stained the pure white page.

It was a feeble attempt to tell a story I didn't write, and a subtle way of holding tight that which He told me to let go. And when the tassels fell from my hands, I realized something I never had before.

Lord Jesus, who am I to deserve such a story?

My daughter, You whisper.

And I believe You.

CHAPTER 10

8 Days

Those who believe that they believe in God,
but without passion in their hearts,
without anguish in mind, without uncertainly,
without doubt, without an element of
despair even in their consolation,
believe in the God idea, not God himself.

~ MIGUEL DE UNAMUNO

I f you were to press me, I would have to say that Thomas was my favorite disciple.

But don't press me. Because it's like the life verse thing and now I'm already thinking of how fond I am of Peter. And John is awesome too. What about least favorite? Can we do that instead? I'm just saying, they all have some good lessons wrapped up in them.

It's unfortunate that Thomas has become known as "the doubter," because if his life with Christ before the resurrection is any indication, he was actually a man of pretty strong faith. Thomas, otherwise known as "Didymus" in Greek, means, "the twin." He can scarcely be mentioned without the word "doubt," as that seems to be the characteristic most often associated with him.

The nickname that is now sometimes used to make a point with others, "Doubting Thomas," is certainly not interpreted as a compliment. He was the one who stubbornly refused to accept that Christ had risen from the dead, despite the fact that all disciples had seen Him. I've painted him in my mind as a near-traitor, denying that which his very closest comrades were trying to convince him.

He didn't mince words in his response to their claims, stating, "Unless I see in his hands the mark of the nails, and place my finger into the mark of the nails, and place my hand into his side, I will never believe" (John 20:25).

Those are some pretty serious boundary lines to draw around your faith, aren't they? "This is the only way I will believe. Period. I don't care about the evidence or the hearsay, I want to physically touch Him with my own hand or I won't accept it as truth."

You're probably familiar with this Thomas, but I want to take you back a few chapters in John's gospel before we let this declaration shape him entirely.

Up until his little rant about needing to see Jesus' hands, we've only met Thomas twice and both instances gave us glimpses of his personality. The first was when Jesus told His disciples He was going to head back to Judea because Lazarus has died. They were resistant, knowing that He was in danger there and would likely be killed.

But Thomas spoke up, declaring, "Let us also go, that we may die with him" (John 11:16).

He obviously trusted the Lord and was willing to put himself in harm's way on His behalf, claiming he would do so even to the point of death if need be. That doesn't sound like someone who is short on faith, does it? *I will die for You if I need to.*

He's the only one who pipes up, so I'm assuming the others weren't as ecstatic about their possible death sentence. Does it surprise you that he was so willing to follow? It surprised me. I've never seen that part happen on a flannel board before. (If you've read my other books, or my blog, or you've had more than a four-minute conversation with me, you'll know I have flannel board envy. I didn't have that growing up and I'm still a little jealous of those who did. Never mind the fact that I just worked my issues into a section about a man who is declaring his allegiance to Jesus even to the point of death. I'm aware of the disconnect, but I appreciate your concern.)

So, we have a different image of Thomas now. He was a loyal follower.

At least, he was a loyal follower as long as he could see the Lord standing in front of him. And maybe Jesus had a hunch that would be the case.

In chapter 14, we start to see his questioning spirit creeping in a little more as Jesus explains that He is going away (alluding to heaven), and that His disciples shouldn't be concerned. He assures them He is preparing a place for them and that He will come back for them, explaining, "You know the way to where I am going" (v. 4).

So Jesus has told them in a nutshell that everything is going to be okay. He doesn't tell them all the specifics, but He urges them to believe instead of being troubled.

I would love to say that would have been enough for me, but I know better. So I'm a little bit relieved that Thomas pipes up, saying, "Lord, we do not know where you are going. How can we know the way?" (v. 5).

I can't help but wonder if he was the unnamed disciple who asked about prayer. It seems like it would be fitting for him.

In other words, he's saying, "I'm not sure I understand what You're telling me to do." He isn't being disrespectful or even blatantly doubting, he's just saying he doesn't comprehend the task. *But he wants to.*

I see an earnestness in him as he questions the Lord, but I don't think it's based on doubt so much as it's his nature to desire clarification.

Have I mentioned I like him? Because I sure do.

Thank You, Lord, for putting a Type A disciple in the bunch.

What we know of Thomas up until this point is that he is a man who trusts Jesus. That's all the information we've been given. So when he says he doesn't know what the Lord is talking about, he's not being sarcastic or speaking down to Jesus.

Essentially he's just saying, *"How will I follow You when I can no longer see Your feet on the path ahead of me?"*

I get that.

Read carefully the two statements we've heard from Thomas: I will risk my life to follow You, but can You tell me **how** to follow You?

Quite frankly, I think Thomas should get credit for one of the best questions ever asked in Scripture.

He's not saying he won't go; he's just saying he doesn't know where he is supposed to go. He's being honest in his concern about what's around the corner, and he's going to ask while he can. I know a lot of people see him as a "glass half empty" kind of guy, but I don't get that feeling when I read about him. I just think he had questions and he wanted Jesus to give him guidance.

How can we know the way?

And here's the beauty of it; Jesus answers his question by redefining the road.

You already know the way. I am the way.

It's not a map; it's a Man.

It's not a direction; it's a Deity.

It's not a path; it's a Person.

It isn't geography you have to know; it's *God*.

Thomas doesn't say another word.

Philip asked to see the Father, declaring that seeing Him would be enough for them to believe. I can't help but smile as Philip essentially asks Jesus to bring in His Dad for show and tell, explaining that this will "suffice" as evidence. Well I should sure hope so, Philip.

Jesus rebukes him (unlike Thomas) and asks Philip how he could have walked beside Him for so long and not know Him.

"How can you say, 'show us the Father'? Do you not believe that I am in the Father and the Father is in me? The words that I say to you I do not speak on my own authority, but the Father who dwells in me does his works. Believe me that I am in the Father and the Father is in me" (vv. 9–11).

Follow Me.

I am the way.

In fairness, Thomas really didn't know where Christ was going. None of us do. We know where He says He is, and we believe Him, but we don't *know* the place. And if it's up to us to find Him there, we need a better set of directions.

But it isn't.

Which is why the Lord explains that He is the way, because our eyes shouldn't be on the ground, looking for bread crumbs that lead to Him.

Because if they are, they aren't beholding that for which they were created to see: *Him.*

We cannot rely on our own fingers and feet to get us there. We have to take Him at His word and trust that He is preparing a place for us. Faith isn't an easy task, not even for those who felt His breath on their faces. And when Christ was crucified, the disciples weren't thinking about Him being resurrected. It wasn't something they understood was going to happen. Even as John and Peter stood in the empty tomb they didn't realize He was going to appear to them again in the flesh. Mary Magdalene was the first to see Him and she told the disciples about her encounter. Later that night, He appeared in the room where they were hiding from the Jews in fear.

I'm just going to throw this out because I think it's something that's important when we're reading Scripture, and maybe it will bless you the way it did me. I've always heard people talk about the fact that Jesus walked through a wall when He came to the disciples. I'm not saying He didn't, or that He couldn't have, but the Bible doesn't in fact tell us that's the case. It says that although the doors were locked, Jesus came and stood among them. So, we don't exactly know how He got in. Did He just open the door as if it wasn't locked? Climb through a window? I don't know, and honestly it really doesn't matter except for the fact that it doesn't say He walked through a wall. That's what other people say, not the Bible.

Don't be intimidated to read Scripture for yourself and ask what the text is saying. There have been times I listened to other people's commentaries without simply reading it myself because I felt I wasn't smart enough to understand it the way they did. I'm not fluent in Greek and I don't have a single Bible-related degree. But He makes His Word accessible to all, and that is good news.

After Jesus entered the locked room, He immediately said, "Peace be with you," (John 20:19) in anticipation of their response. He knew they were probably going to be a little thrown by the fact that He was right there, and I love that He started it off by saying, "It's okay. Have peace in place of your fear."

With that, He shows them His hands and His side, still marred from His brutal death. Obviously He could have healed them fully, but He chose not to for their (and our) sake. He wanted to assure them He was the same Christ they had followed—the Christ who had overcome the grave. He wanted them to see evidence of the miracle.

Scripture tells us of how glad the disciples were to be in His presence and no doubt they were overwhelmed by the reality that He is indeed the God He claimed to be.

Have you ever stopped to consider the fact that Jesus chose to come at a time when Thomas wasn't there?

It wasn't an accident. He is the God of the universe. I'm pretty sure He knows when people step out for a bit. He knew that Thomas was not there.

And He knew that Thomas would doubt.

Thomas would not take their word for it. Plain and simple.

There's a part of me that applauds him instead of seeing him as obstinate. Other people's experience of Jesus was not satisfactory and he made no bones about it.

I will have to see Him for myself. I will have to put my own hands inside the wounds you claim you saw in order for it to be my belief.

Eight days went by with no sign of Him and then suddenly, in the same room, the Lord came and stood before them. But this time, Thomas was present.

Upon entering, Christ used the same greeting He had before, "Peace be with you" (v. 26).

Next come words that bring tears to my eyes. Words that say more than almost anything else in times when I see myself as a failure because I have uncertainty.

"Then He said to Thomas . . ."

Our Lord—our tender, loving, ever-gracious Lord—turned to the one disciple who was the least convinced and *He spoke directly to him.* He wasn't angry. He wasn't calling him out on his sinful lack of trust; He came to Thomas to speak face-to-face with him out of love.

Do you remember at the beginning of our journey together, when I talked so much about understanding love as the motivation behind all of God's work? We see this displayed powerfully as He comes back for the one who does love Him but didn't know *how to love Him.*

I can hardly stand it.

Thomas was chasing God, making up his own rules and requirements. And although I can't know for certain Jesus' motivation, it seems that the Lord couldn't stand for him to live that way, and instead of leaving clues, He came back.

He came back.

"Put your finger here, and see my hands; and put out your hand, and place it in my side. Do not disbelieve, but believe" (v. 27).

While both what Thomas and Jesus said is translated into most of our English translations with the word "put," the original Greek words they used are different. When Thomas says he won't believe without putting his hand in Christ's side, the word he used was *ballo*, which means "to put in or insert." Other definitions of the same word say that it means to let something go without caring where it falls. But when Christ invited Thomas to do so, the word used was *phero*, which, while used to indicate the act of reaching the hand forth, places an emphasis on Thomas's responsibility. Other definitions used for the word *phero* suggest he is asking Thomas "to bear or to carry a burden." So, Thomas had said that he would have to essentially touch the wound, whereas in response Jesus calls Him not just to touch, but rather to bear the burden of the wound.

You do your part and I'll do Mine.

But, Lord . . . what is my part? I don't know the way . . .

How, Lord? How do I follow You?

I'll tell you this. There are few moments recorded in all of Scripture that have moved me and shaped my heart more than what happened next.

Thomas had made it clear that nothing less than touching the risen Christ would make him believe.

Nothing.

And here was Jesus, steps away from him, inviting him to do exactly that.

But it was not the sound of Thomas's feet that broke the silence.

It was his voice.

"My Lord and my God!"

It is the first time anyone in the New Testament calls Jesus God.

Thomas is lost in truth, swallowed entirely by the grace given to him. He is so unaware of himself that it seems he forgets his required task. Or maybe he realizes he doesn't need to chase God anymore. I've seen it depicted in art dozens of times, and I've resisted standing up and embarrassing myself in sermons, but the truth of the matter is this: Scripture gives us no reason to believe Thomas ever actually touched Jesus.

Do you hear that? Does it make you smile like it does me? Do you hear your own voice in the conversations?

"This is what I need to do in order to believe."

"Unless this happens, I will doubt."

"There is no way I'm going to trust God until He . . ."

I know.

I've thought them if not said them. I have my conditions, Lord. And I will be loyal and whole-heartedly devoted to You if You will just let me have that assurance. It's an if-then sometimes, isn't it? If I touch the wounds, then I will be healed.

And He is kind to lead us to our own mistake—the one that stops our feet in their tracks.

No, daughter; the wounds have already healed you.

There is nowhere to step, nowhere to grasp, and nowhere to chase.

He stands before us, telling us He hears our doubts and He knows our requirements. And yet He knows more than what we really need and that is what He offers.

Stand still and behold Me instead of trying to satisfy yourself, and you will find that I am enough. Go ahead and draw your lines in the sand if it makes you feel better. Shout your requests to the sky and tell everyone else you can't be sure. If that's what you need to do, then do it. Because I know it comes from a heart that wants to find Me. And sooner or later, you'll look up. And you'll realize you've been staring down at the path so long you forgot who it was you were following.

I will come to you and I will remind you. Your defenses will fall like a rainy night, and you'll stand in awe of Me.

It isn't the way.

I am.

You don't have to chase God in order to believe God.

Look up, take Him in, and acknowledge His majesty with the mouth you used to question Him. He is here where He has always been, but you've been so busy with the chase that you didn't recognize Him.

I don't want to run anymore; I want to kneel.

"Then He said to Thomas . . ."

I read those words over and over and I feel the tears sting and the foundation feels solid again. He invites me to touch His side, pierced on my behalf, and I would be tempted to be ashamed of my own doubt if it wasn't for His display of affection.

And thus it frequently happens that a
man who has vowed that he will not believe
except this or that be made plain finds, when
he does believe, that something short of his
own requirements has convinced him. He
finds that though he was once so express in
his demands for proof, and so clear and accu-
rate in his declarations of the precise amount
of evidence required, at the last he believes
and could scarcely tell you why, could not
at least show his belief as the fine and clean
result of a logical process. Thomas had main-
tained that the rest were too easily satisfied,
but at the last he is himself satisfied with pre-
cisely the same proof as they. And it is somewhat striking that in so many cases unbelief
gives way to belief, not by the removal of
intellectual difficulties, not by such demon-
stration as was granted to Thomas, but by an
undefinable conquest of the soul by Christ.
The glory, holiness, love of His person, sub-
due the soul to Him.[20]

For years, I have said something not unlike this to God: "I
believe You. But I'm not sure how to follow You. This is what
You need to do to convince me."

What I had never considered, and I'm willing to bet
Thomas hadn't either, was that He would take me up on it.

I wanted to catch up with Him, but I never thought about the consequence. I wanted to touch the imprint of the nails without acknowledging I held the hammer. I wanted my hand inside the wound, proving to me He was real, but I refused to be the one responsible.

We would rather chase the God who rose victoriously than behold the One wounded on our behalf. And finally I realized the difference, and I, like Thomas, stood still. Perfectly still.

And when I stand still, I see Your robe fill the temple.

I hear the sound of Your voice, and I can't help but shake in awe.

I would have kept running, Lord. But that wasn't the answer.

So You came back for me; to remind me that You loved me that much.

And You whispered the words that quarried me deep:

Stop looking for Me, love. Look at Me.

He came back for Thomas. He came back for me.

He may come to the side of a barren sea, telling you He sees something you don't. But you are going to have to put the net down if you want to see the miracle for yourself.

He may turn around in the midst of a crowd and tell you He knows your name and that, despite your disease, He loves you and sees you as healed.

He might even answer a prayer you had, inviting your very hand to touch the mystery.

But I'll speak from experience—*you won't dare.*

You will realize the sound of your feet has been quieted, and you'll scarcely dream of looking anywhere but here, where He has always been.

No more chasing. It isn't the way.

He is.

You'll wonder how you've relied on your own efforts this long, and you'll lift the alabaster box as high as your hands can reach, smashing it to the ground while you look deep into the sacred wound that brought you life.

And the words, like perfume, will spill into the silence:

My Lord, and my God . . . here am I.

Notes

1. *Blue Letter Bible*, "Dictionary and Word Search for *radaph (Strong's 7291)*," (1996–2013), http://www.blueletterbible.org/lang/lexicon/lexicon.cfm?strongs=H7291.

2. Ibid., "*akoloutheō* (Strong's 190)," http://www.blueletterbible.org/lang/lexicon/lexicon.cfm?Strongs=G190.

3. Ibid., "*horaō* (Strong's 3708)," http://www.blueletterbible.org/lang/lexicon/lexicon.cfm?strongs=G3708.

4. *Calvin's Commentaries*, Volume 7 (Ada, MI: Baker Books, 2005), 213–14.

5. *Blue Letter Bible*, "*synechō (Strong's 4912)*," http:// www.blueletterbible.org/lang/lexicon/lexicon.cfm?strongs=4912.

6. C. S. Lewis, *Mere Christianity* (San Francisco, CA: Harper San Francisco, 2009), 117.

7. Hannah Whitall Smith, *The God of All Comfort* (Chicago, IL: Moody Publishers, 1953), 44.

8. M. R. Mulholland Jr., *Invitation to a Journey* (Downers Grove, IL: InterVarsity Press, 1993), 133.

9. Lewis, *Mere Christianity*, 117–18.

10. R. C. Sproul, *Now That's a Good Question* (Wheaton, IL: Tyndale, 1996), 156–57.

11. John MacArthur Jr., *Alone with God* (Colorado Springs: David C. Cook, 2011), 61.

12. Paula Rinehart, *Strong Women, Soft Hearts* (Nashville: Thomas Nelson, 2005), 118.

13. D. Martyn Lloyd-Jones, *Studies in the Sermon on the Mount* (Grand Rapids, MI: Eerdmans, 1984), 387.

14. Rinehart, *Strong Women, Soft Hearts,* 119.

15.Alexander McClaren, from the sermon entitled "Faith Tested and Crowned."

16. Jean Fleming, *Feeding Your Soul* (Colorado Springs: NavPress, 1999), 79.

17. See www.kjvtoday.com/home/only-begotten-or-one-and -only-in-john-316-et-al.

18. *Blue Letter Bible, ra'ah (Strong's 7200),*" http://www. blueletterbible.org/lang/lexicon/lexicon.cfm?strongs=H7200.

19. John Calvin, *Commentary on a Harmony of the Evangelists, Matthew, Mark, and Luke,* Volume 2 (Grand Rapids, MI: Eerdmans, 1949), 304.

20. William R. Nicoll, *Expositor's Bible Commentary,* http:// www.studylight.org/com/teb/view.cgi?bk=42&ch=20.

Also Available
by
ANGIE SMITH

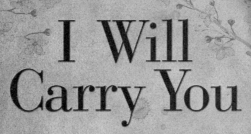

I Will
Carry You

The Sacred Dance of Grief and Joy

Angie Smith

978-0-8054-6428-3

The sweet and powerful story of Angie's baby girl who changed the world and whose story helps us all understand how better to cope with loss and disappointment.

Every WORD Matters®
BHPublishingGroup.com

Also Available
by
ANGIE SMITH

978-0-8054-6429-0

Journey with Angie as she walks you
through the biblical stories of others
who have simultaneously loved God and
struggled with faith-so that He will be
glorified and you will be transformed!

Every WORD Matters®
BHPublishingGroup.com

Also Available
by
ANGIE SMITH

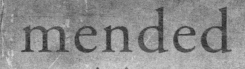

mended

pieces of a life made whole

ANGIE SMITH

"God speaks hope, help, and healing through Angie and does it so endearingly and even so humorously that you let your guard down and receive, even before you meant to."
—BETH MOORE

978-1-4336-7660-4

Mended takes you on a journey to show how faith lived in the regular events of daily life is all that it takes to be a part of creating God's picture of redemption in your life and those around you.

B&H
Every WORD Matters®
BHPublishingGroup.com

AngieSmithOnline.com

To learn more about Angie Smith's books, her blog, and her speaking events, check out AngieSmithOnline.com

Bring the Rain